T0353347

Aligning Perceptual and Conceptual Information for Cognitive Contextual System Development:

Emerging Research and Opportunities

Gary Kuvich
IBM, USA

A volume in the Advances in
Systems Analysis, Software
Engineering, and High Performance
Computing (ASASEHPC) Book Series

Published in the United States of America by
    IGI Global
    Engineering Science Reference (an imprint of IGI Global)
    701 E. Chocolate Avenue
    Hershey PA, USA 17033
    Tel: 717-533-8845
    Fax: 717-533-8661
    E-mail: cust@igi-global.com
    Web site: http://www.igi-global.com

Library of Congress Cataloging-in-Publication Data

Names: Kuvich, Gary, 1960- author.
Title: Aligning perceptual and conceptual information for cognitive
    contextual system development : emerging research and opportunities / by
    Gary Kuvich.
Description: Hershey, PA : Engineering Science Reference, [2017]
Identifiers: LCCN 2017010703| ISBN 9781522524311 (hardcover) | ISBN
    9781522524328 (ebook)
Subjects: LCSH: Artificial intelligence. | Cognitive science. | Automation. |
    Perceptual learning.
Classification: LCC TA347.A78 K89 2017 | DDC 006.3--dc23 LC record available at https://lccn.
loc.gov/2017010703

This book is published in the IGI Global book series Advances in Systems Analysis, Software Engineering, and High Performance Computing (ASASEHPC) (ISSN: 2327-3453; eISSN: 2327-3461)

British Cataloguing in Publication Data
A Cataloguing in Publication record for this book is available from the British Library.

All work contributed to this book is new, previously-unpublished material.
The views expressed in this book are those of the authors, but not necessarily of the publisher.

For electronic access to this publication, please contact: eresources@igi-global.com.

Advances in Systems Analysis, Software Engineering, and High Performance Computing (ASASEHPC) Book Series

ISSN:2327-3453
EISSN:2327-3461

Editor-in-Chief: Vijayan Sugumaran Oakland University, USA

MISSION

The theory and practice of computing applications and distributed systems has emerged as one of the key areas of research driving innovations in business, engineering, and science. The fields of software engineering, systems analysis, and high performance computing offer a wide range of applications and solutions in solving computational problems for any modern organization.

The **Advances in Systems Analysis, Software Engineering, and High Performance Computing (ASASEHPC) Book Series** brings together research in the areas of distributed computing, systems and software engineering, high performance computing, and service science. This collection of publications is useful for academics, researchers, and practitioners seeking the latest practices and knowledge in this field.

COVERAGE

- Software engineering
- Parallel Architectures
- Enterprise information systems
- Engineering Environments
- Computer Networking
- Performance Modelling
- Distributed Cloud Computing
- Network Management
- Human-computer interaction
- Metadata and Semantic Web

IGI Global is currently accepting manuscripts for publication within this series. To submit a proposal for a volume in this series, please contact our Acquisition Editors at Acquisitions@igi-global.com or visit: http://www.igi-global.com/publish/.

Titles in this Series

For a list of additional titles in this series, please visit:
https://www.igi-global.com/book-series/advances-systems-analysis-software-engineering/73689

For an enitre list of titles in this series, please visit:
https://www.igi-global.com/book-series/advances-systems-analysis-software-engineering/73689

701 East Chocolate Avenue, Hershey, PA 17033, USA
Tel: 717-533-8845 x100 • Fax: 717-533-8661
E-Mail: cust@igi-global.com • www.igi-global.com

Table of Contents

Preface

INTRODUCTION

The audience for this book is industry practitioners and startup workers in the areas of robotics, unmanned vehicles, machine perception, and cognitive applications. These areas are now rapidly moving from research into industrial applications, forming large and profitable industries. Certain obstacles have created a bottleneck for that in the past, and they have to be removed for this transformation to happen successfully at this time.

Robots need senses similar to human vision in its unique capabilities to extract and understand meaningful information from the surrounding environment. And it has become clear that robotic perception requires a context system that is provided by the cognition in nature. Robotic intelligence needs to be smart enough if we really want anything practical out of it.

One of the primary reasons caused the bottleneck is a gap between the low-level recognition methods, and high level cognitive semantic models of AI. This gap existed for decades and is still there.

Recognition works as "learning-recall," and existing recognition models are based on the flavors of adaptive statistical learning. Natural phenomena that support adaptive statistics are well known and backed by the neuroscience.

Learning and recall are how our memory works. But it doesn't do any abstract intelligent operation that we human are good at, which distinct us from animals. Learning and recall mechanism can only be a part of human intelligence. So-called "deep learning" still works as a more advanced version of "learning-recall." So, recent advances in "deep learning" didn't really change anything in the existing gap.

We can process raw perceptual information much further, deriving order and abstract structures in it. This is equivalent to our ability to understand. In many cases, this also helps us to disambiguate raw input information unconsciously. We can make quick, intelligent decisions upon the abstracted perceptual information and additional contextual cognitive knowledge. And we can create plans and other abstract cognitive models to enrich our knowledge base and store it in the memory.

Existing cognitive semantic models are based on the logics and symbols. The neural or cortical mechanisms that may support such models are not known. And such models remain purely artificial mathematical constructs. Problems and shortcomings of such models arise from their artificial nature. We may not guarantee that such models are actually capable of doing all needed intelligent operations from the above paragraph. And unfortunately, that has already been proven many times in past.

Due to a multiplicity of perceptual and cognitive processes, and complexity of the subject, the author doesn't believe that the solution may be presented as a single mathematical theory. A single mathematical theory usually covers a family of similar methods that stemmed from its postulates. But we may need methods from different mathematical areas.

Perceptual and cognitive processes in the brain apparently comprise a multilevel informational hierarchy with multiple feedbacks between the levels. And due to this nature, author believes that the solution should be presented rather in the form of some architecture, where perceptual and cognitive models have a unified basis for working together in a single system; they are capable of both doing intelligent operations and accumulating knowledge; and they have at least a certain analogy with cortical and neural mechanisms, which is now lacking in the semantic models.

Our perception works with continuous raw information, and it can recognize similar patterns in the input data, identify order and structures in it, and disambiguate perceptual information using a context system from higher levels. Most of the perceptual processes are subconscious.

Our cognitive system uses crisp conceptual information on its top levels. And such processes are conscious. This led scientists to the semantic cognitive models that are based on the concepts of human language, logics, and symbols.

In reality, there is no any clear crisp border between perception and cognition. They are different levels of a single multilevel system with feedbacks between the levels.

At a certain point after training, recognition is making a clear response - the decision about the particular input pattern, choosing one from a finite number of similar patterns. And this decision denotes a recognized pattern for the next levels of hierarchy.

So the entire recognition mechanism converts input information into the set of discrete answers. On the higher level, this is equivalent to an alphabet with a finite set of symbols, where each symbol denotes a distinctive pattern.

A single universal recognizer is a dangerous idea. It would be very ineffective from the computational standpoint, and neuroscience doesn't support it either. There might be an infinite number of such alphabets with expandable but finite sets of similar patterns.

This is how implicit perceptual symbols may emerge in the system. From that point, such a symbol may leave its own life on the higher levels, and establish links with other symbols, forming meaningful structures and discrete patterns. Such structures are mimicking order of the world.

And this is where our intelligence emerges. It is pretty obvious that brain may work with graphs and diagrammatic-like structures. So instead of semantic models that are restricted to human language constructs, we would rather use graphs and diagrammatic models as a basis for the intelligent models.

Nodes of the graphs or diagrams can link into a pattern. Such a pattern can be recognized and creates its symbol, which will be used as a node of the graph on the next level. The same rule applies on the higher levels related to cognition.

Therefore, we can create new implicit symbols on fly both from the perceptual and conceptual information. We can bind them into meaningful structures. We can use these structures as patterns, which will have their symbols. This creates a compact world model, which can be implemented in modern computers in the same way.

All of this is already supported by the neuroscience. And we can make the final step: graph transformations are needed for some intelligent operations. We may suggest that some learned patterns allow us doing such transformations mentally. Then we could have explanations for the planning, and other intellectual capabilities.

In opposition to Semantic approach, author calls this approach as Cognitive Semiotics, because Semiotics is a science of Signs and Symbols that stand for something. Traditional Semiotics studies visual signs. That has no practical value for the purpose of this book, and Cognitive Semiotics has nothing to do with the Traditional one.

ORGANIZATION OF BOOK

This book is organized in the following chapters.

The introduction describes the past that led to the existing situation, providing a brief overview.

Chapter 1

"Cognitive Semiotics and the Game of Life" briefly describe overall architectural requirements to the Autonomous Systems, and provides details on:

- How implicit perceptual symbols emerge in the brain,
- Evidence from neuroscience,
- Mathematical methods that can generate implicit symbols from perceptual information.

Chapter 2

"Topological Semiotic Knowledge Representation" describes cognitive models that organize implicit symbols into meaningful relational network structures. With an understanding of implicit symbols, there is evidence that informational processes on the cortical level can create and maintain multileveled hierarchically nested graphs and diagram – like structures.

This topological model reflects hierarchically ordered knowledge of world structure and processes. The author calls such models Network-Symbolic. Such networks have nothing to do with neural networks or single neurons.

Semantic network models are most close to an understanding of such models. But semantic networks are tightly bound to language constructs, and they lacked the flexibility of creating new symbols and structures on the fly, missing middle levels of perceptual cognitive hierarchy.

Suggested Network-Symbolic models reflect systems, and they have structural relations embedded in the model. Ability to generate on fly new meaningful graphs and diagrams allows for modeling phenomena of intelligence like analogies, conceptual blending, and many others.

Chapter 3

"Driving Mechanisms and Patterns" briefly touches role of positive and negative feedback mechanisms that are similar to emotion, and can drive processes to reach goals.

Chapter 4

"Semiotics of Visual Information" explains how active vision and image understanding can be implemented with such architecture and models.

Chapter 5

"Practical Implementation" briefly touches APIs that could be used today for implementing of proposed architecture and methods.

Computer scientists, working in the same areas, might find this book interesting. Cognitive scientists may also benefit from this book, considering some suggestions of what informational phenomena they may be looking for.

Introduction

Within the past 15 years, the area of unmanned vehicles and robotics application was growing exponentially. That usually happens when some technologies are rapidly converting from research into industry.

In the first decade of 21st Century, most of modern unmanned vehicles and robots were remotely controlled by operators. However, despite significant achieved success, operator control can efficiently work for individual missions. But it is tough to provide a rapidly growing fleet of unmanned vehicles with efficient remote control by human operators.

And, even worse, the communication channels may be vulnerable to the means of electronic interception. A high tech enemy may relatively easy jeopardize the entire remotely controlled mission. So, the autonomic situation awareness and smart decision making according to the mission goals are vital not only for the new robotic products on the rapidly growing markets. But this applies also to the new generation of UAVs and UGVs.

Autonomous perceptual systems of the robotic and unmanned vehicles must carry a large payload, and they have expanded requirements for fast and reliable interpretation of sensor data. Infra-red and other kinds of modern sensors can see beyond the human senses. But nothing yet can replace human vision in its unique ability to understand and interpret visual information.

For many years, the automation of human-like image processing was thought of only as a solution to the Pattern Recognition Problem. Various people in different countries, involved in the development of such systems, observed an interesting phenomenon. The system usually performed well on the test samples. But under field conditions, the performance was always sharply degraded.

The reasons for all of that are more serious than the lack of appropriate ideas or imprecision of the methods. Vision is only a part of a larger informational system that converts visual information into knowledge structures. These structures drive the vision process, resolving ambiguity and uncertainty via feedback, and provide image understanding, which is an interpretation of visual information regarding these knowledge models. It is hard to split the entire system apart.

In the human vision, the scene context plays a significant role in the identification of the target. In many cases, an object can only be recognized correctly after identification of its role/position in the scene. Separating of an image on target and clutter might simply not be feasible before this.

The reliable solutions to the Pattern Recognition Problems are possible only within the settlement of a more generic Image Understanding Problem. Vision mechanisms can never be completely understood apart from the informational processes related to knowledge and intelligence. Failure of modern computer vision systems is a failure of their knowledge components.

Imagine a situation in which you will need to provide your developers with the project specs for an intelligent system with scene understanding capabilities.

The biggest problems are not about the lack of methods and algorithms. The major questions are: what to use, why, and how. Should you choose Neural Networks, HMMs, Fuzzy Sets, or some other methods? When would certain ways be preferable to others? And how relevant are these methods to the solution of your problems? And, more importantly, what schemas will bring them together into a real vision system?

Finding such answers requires a theory that can explain how humans understand and interpret real-world images at a level that allows for a computer simulation. Such an approach is called Cognitive Semiotics. This book describes the theory and focuses on the implementation details.

Author initial intention was to provide in this book a deep analysis of what happened in the area of computer intelligence and cognition. But it appeared that this has already been done in the excellent book of Hawkins and Blakeslee (2004), *On Intelligence*. They did it so nicely that instead of just referring readers to his book, I will give some short review and will use his exact citations in multiple places. I believe that it is very relevant to the topic of this book, and is worth to bring it here. However, there are certain places where my vision of the problem and solution is significantly or entirely different.

Per Hawkins, intelligent machines will arise from a new set of principles about the nature of intelligence:

A mountain of data about the brain was collected over hundreds of years, and the rate at which we are gathering more data is accelerating. The United States alone has thousands of neuroscientists. But despite everything, there are no productive theories about what intelligence is or how the brain works as a whole. (Hawkins & Blakeslee, 2004, p. 2)

Hawkins believes that this is because of misunderstanding differences between basic principles of brains and computers. But this difference is so obvious that no one thinks today that brain and computer work in the same way.

I would say something different. The real cause, in my opinion, is that core mathematical principle of informational processes in the human brain and cognition are still not well understood.

There were multiple efforts from Computer scientists to program computers to act like humans without first answering what intelligence is and what it means "to understand." That led to the situations, where a few fragmentary artificial methods, capable of solving some limited intelligent problems positioned as no less as the entire "Artificial Intelligence."

It was picked up and widely advertised by the popular media. And nothing is surprising that it appeared clearly that such methods are not capable of solving many other problems that real Artificial Intelligence was expected to address (Hawkins & Blakeslee, 2004).

And it created an enormous frustration and disappointment in the so-called "Artificial Intelligence." It has now a similar degree of credibility as the famous "Philosopher's Stone" – a legendary substance, allegedly capable of turning inexpensive metals into gold in the Middle Ages Alchemy. By that reason, many industry practitioners are now just avoiding using this name.

Hawkins describes this situation very nicely:

In all cases, the successful AI programs were only good at the one particular thing for which they were specifically designed. They didn't generalize or show flexibility, and even their creators admitted they didn't think like humans. Some AI problems, which at first were thought to be easy, yielded no progress. Even today, no computer can understand language as well as a three-year-old or see as well as a mouse.

After many years of effort, unfulfilled promises, and no unqualified successes, AI started to lose its luster. Scientists in the field moved on to other areas of research. AI start-up companies failed. And funding became scarcer. (Hawkins & Blakeslee, 2004, p. 18)

Hawkins correctly described the root of the situation with AI. Demonstrating samples of intelligent-like behavior don't prove that system has the same flexibility as human intelligence. Artificial Turing tests may work around the subject. In this sense, the uncut version of Terminator movie with Schwarzenegger is a perfect example of how to pass Turing test without much intelligence.

In the uncut version episode, the Terminator is sitting in a locked room when the landlord comes to collect rent from his tenants. And he is talking to the Terminator across the closed door and walls. And the landlord doesn't know that he is talking not to a human, but to an intelligent machine, which resembles the conditions for a Turing Test.

In respond to the landlord demand, a menu from 3 optional answers shows up in the Terminator's brain: 1. Yes, 2. No, and 3. Something very vulgar. Cursor slides down to the third menu option, Terminator chooses it, says it aloud in a loud rude voice, and the landlord leaves. Great, the intelligent machine had overcome human and passed the Turing Test! But does this require a human level of intelligence?

The author worked on the Artificial Life project, where we as a group of enthusiasts were trying to build a small conversational system. The chat agent was able to talk like a human, and you may not find any difference. But the conversation was literally about nothing, because for a meaningful conversation we human use a context domain knowledge that was completely lacking in the system.

Efforts to make computers intelligent will be failing until there is no viable theory how cognition processes may work on the level, which would allow modeling such processes on the computers.

Hawkins pointed that the best way to solve the problem is to use the detailed biology of the brain as a constraint and as a guide, yet think about intelligence as a computational problem. The real solution is somewhere between biology and computer science. Many biologists ignore the idea of thinking of the brain in computational terms, and computer scientists often don't believe they have anything to learn from biology.

Hawkins provided a comprehensive theory of how the brain works. It describes what intelligence is and how human brain may create it. He gathered in a coherent fashion many of the individual ideas that existed in some form before, but not together.

Hawkins makes the point that before we attempt to build intelligent machines; we have first to understand how the brain thinks in terms of information and system sciences.

He introduced and developed the core idea of the theory of memory-prediction framework. Analyzing situation in that area, Hawkins noticed that for many years, scientists in the field of artificial intelligence have claimed that computers will be intelligent when they are powerful enough. But computer power and capacity per se may not provide intelligence.

Another assumption was that neural networks supposed to lead to intelligent machines. But that promise has never been delivered. And Hawkins is nicely describing this situation:

Around this time, a new and promising approach to thinking about intelligent machines burst onto the scene. Neural networks had been around since the late 1960s in one form or another, but neural networks and the AI movement were competitors, for both the dollars and the mind share of the agencies that fund research. AI, the 800-pound gorilla in those days, actively squelched neural network research. Neural network researchers were essentially blacklisted from getting funding for several years. A few people continued to think about them though, and in the mid-1980s their day in the sun had finally arrived. It is hard to know exactly why there was a sudden interest in neural networks, but undoubtedly one contributing factor was the continuing failure of artificial intelligence. People were casting about for alternatives to AI and found one in artificial neural networks. (Hawkins & Blakeslee, 2004, p. 24)

Neural networks architecture mimics certain aspects of real nervous systems. Neural network researchers, a.k.a. connectionists, were interested in learning about behaviors, exhibited by connecting of models of neurons together.

On a top level, the brain consists of neurons. In the same way, we could say that a computer is a silicon machine. It is correct but won't bring us to our goal any close.

The hope of connectionists was that the intelligence would become apparent by studying how neurons interact and solve problems that were unsolvable with AI by replicating the right connections between populations of neurons.

Neural networks have two powerful inspirational sources from other disciplines: adaptive statistics in math, and Hebbian learning phenomenon from Neuroscience. The neural network's knowledge and memories distributed throughout its connectivity—just like real brains.

Per Hawkins and Blakeslee (2004), the following things are essential to understanding the brain:

- Time in brain function.
- Feedback connections everywhere in the brain. Examples:
  - ◦ Connections going backward toward the input exceed the connections going forward by almost a factor between the neocortex and the thalamus.
  - ◦ The ratio of every fiber feeding information forward into the neocortex to fibers feeding information back toward the senses is approximately one to ten.
  - ◦ Feedback dominates most connections throughout the neocortex. The precise role of this feedback is not entirely understood. But it existed everywhere.

But the mainstream of neural network phenomenon settled on a class of ultra simple models, and none of those criteria were. Most models consisted of a small number of neurons connected in a few layers. A data pattern is applied to the first input row. Input neurons attached to the next row of neurons - so-called hidden units. The hidden units then connect to the output units - last row of neurons. By changing the connection strengths, the network learns to map input patterns to output responses.

As Hawkins said:

These simple neural networks only processed static patterns, did not use feedback, and didn't look anything like brains. The most common type of neural network called a "back propagation" network, learned by broadcasting an error from the output units back toward the input units. That feedback only occurred during the learning phase, unlike the real one that is always there. There is no feedback from outputs to inputs during the regular work.

A static input pattern got converted into a static output pattern. Then another input pattern was presented. There was no history or record of the network of what happened even a short time earlier.

And the architecture of these neural networks is simplistic compared to the complicated and hierarchical structure of the brain.

These simple neural networks were able to do adaptive statistics, and "research seemed to stop right there, for years. They had found a new and exciting tool, and overnight thousands of scientists, engineers, and students were getting grants, earning PhDs, and writing books about neural networks.

Companies were formed to use neural networks to predict the stock market, process loan applications, verify signatures, and perform hundreds of other pattern classification applications. Although the intent of the founders of the field might have been more general, the field became dominated by people who weren't interested in understanding how the brain works or understanding what intelligence is.

The popular press didn't understand this distinction well. Newspapers, magazines, and TV science programs presented neural networks as being "brain-like" or working on the "same principles as the brain." Unlike AI, where everything had to be programmed, neural nets learned by example, which seemed, well, somehow more intelligent. (Hawkins & Blakeslee, 2004, p. 27)

Hawkins gave an excellent analogy to show how far neural networks were from real brains:

Imagine that instead of trying to figure out how a brain worked we were trying to figure out how a digital computer worked. After years of study, we discover that everything in the computer is made of transistors. There are hundreds of millions of transistors on a computer, and they are connected in precise and complex ways. But we don't understand how the computer works or why the transistors are connected the way they are. So one day we decide to connect just a few transistors together to see what happens. Later we find that as few as three transistors, when connected in a certain way, become an amplifier. A small signal put into one end is magnified on the other end. (Amplifiers in radios and televisions are made using transistors in this fashion.) This is an important discovery, and overnight an industry springs up making transistor radios, televisions, and other electronic appliances using transistor amplifiers. This is all well and good, but it doesn't tell us anything about how the computer works. Even though an amplifier and a computer are both made of transistors, they have almost nothing else in common. In the same way, a real brain and a three-row neural network are built with neurons, but have almost nothing else in common. (Hawkins & Blakeslee, 2004, p. 27)

Other methods easily handled most of the simple neural networks capabilities, and the media subsided. The neural network researchers never claim their models were intelligent. These simple networks did less than AI programs.

Modern neural networks describe a diverse set of models. Some of which are more biologically accurate and some of which are not. But almost none of them attempt to capture the overall function or architecture of the neocortex.

Per Hawkins, the most fundamental problem with both neural networks and AI programs is that they are focused on behavior. Hawkins raised an interesting philosophical question, noticing that building human and making intelligent machines are two different things:

Being human and being intelligent are separate matters. An intelligent machine need not have sexual urges, hunger, a pulse, muscles, emotions, or a humanlike body.

To build machines that are undoubtedly intelligent but not exactly like humans, we can focus on the part of the brain strictly related to intelligence. (Hawkins & Blakeslee, 2004, p. 41)

Without understanding the brain first, simple neural networks aren't more successful at creating intelligent machines than computer programs have been.

A very brilliant Hawkins's thought is that Complexity is a symptom of confusion, not a cause. Instead, he argued that a few intuitive but incorrect assumptions mislead us. The biggest mistake was the belief that intelligent behavior defines intelligence.

Some people still believe that faster computers can solve AI's problems. But most scientists think the entire endeavor was flawed. The brain creates a model of the world in memory, and that model stores everything that was learned. The purpose of this memory-based model is to make predictions of future events. And the ability to make such predictions is the crux of intelligence.

Hawkins nicely described different approaches between the various groups of researchers from different fields:

Numerous people from many fields had written extensively about thinking and intelligence. Each field had its set of journals, and each used its terminology. I found their descriptions inconsistent and incomplete. Linguists talked of intelligence in terms such as "syntax" and "semantics." To them, the brain and intelligence were all about language. Vision scientists referred to 2D, 2¹ᐟ² D, and 3D sketches. To them, the brain and intelligence were all about visual pattern recognition. Computer scientists talked of schemas and frames, new terms they made up to represent knowledge. None of these people talked about the structure of the brain and how it would implement any of their theories.

On the other hand, anatomists and neurophysiologists wrote extensively about the structure of the brain and how neurons behave, but they mostly avoided any attempt at large-scale theory. It was difficult and frustrating trying to make sense of these various approaches and the mountain of experimental data that accompanied them. (Hawkins & Blakeslee, 2004, p. 24)

It is a well-known fact that different parts of the neocortex are responsible for vision, hearing, touch, or language. Interestingly, though that the neocortex is surprisingly regular in its structural details, and this all work on the same principles.

It means that differences in the processing of information may not be found on the physiological level. And there is something else that makes such informational processes working so differently. Per Hawkins, the key to understanding the neocortex is understanding these universal principles and, in particular, its hierarchical structure.

A significant contribution from Hawkins is that their work has nicely explained how the neocortex structure captures the structure of the world:

Any theory or model of the brain should account for the physical architecture of the brain. The neocortex is not a simple structure. ... it is organized as a repeating hierarchy. Any neural network that didn't knowledge this structure was certainly not going to work like a brain. (Hawkins & Blakeslee, 2004, p. 25)

Per Hawkins, auto-associative memory networks came much closer to describing how real brains work. They are interconnected using lots of feedback. Instead of only passing information forward, as in a regular backpropagation network, auto-associative memories fed the output of each neuron back into the input. Artificial neurons form a memory of the pattern of activity, which was imposed on the input. The auto-associative network associated patterns with themselves, hence the term auto-associative memory.

When presented with part of the sequence, the memory can recall the rest. Hawkins proposed that brain uses circuits similar to an auto-associative memory to do so. Auto-associative memories implement feedback and may work with time-changing inputs. But, unfortunately, this research didn't attract proper attention.

Per Hawkins's observation, the mainstream of neuroscience tend to chart the brain regarding where things happen, not when or how neural firing patterns interact over time. Partially, that comes from the limits of the current experimental techniques. And although in recent years, belief in the importance of feedback, time, and prediction has been on the rise, "The thunder of AI and classical neural networks kept other approaches subdued and underappreciated for many years" (Hawkins, 2004, p. 32).

Hawkins had made many very valid points in his book, like for instance that understanding of intelligence cannot be achieved without an understanding of the principles how the brain processes information. And author agrees with most of the points he made.

But author of this book doesn't believe that it is possible to prove anything just by challenging the views of other influential groups that drove the mainstream and failed. Any argument per se may not be sufficient to prove or disprove anything. The arguments between scientific camps may continue for centuries. One camp may argue that flying a plane is not possible. And they will provide a consistent set of arguments that may convince everyone that a plane could never fly.

In the same way, another camp will be providing another set of logical arguments, which may prove that flying plane is indeed possible. And this saga may continue for centuries. Until someone like Brothers Wright, ignoring all the arguments will find ways that can make the plane fly, and build a prototype. Then the case is closed.

Another word, the real resolution of any argument is a useful practical application.

Author is very thankful to J. Hawkins for a nice analysis how intelligence may work. And this is not a matter of priority in bringing this to the public first. Even if anyone had similar ideas, author doubts that they could express it any better, providing such convincing arguments. Some details may be questioned. But the overall explanations are very convincing.

Hawkins has correctly described natural phenomena, but the ways of building intelligent machines may be different. There are two possible approaches:

1.   Invest in the development of a brain-like environment. It may work pretty well for conditions of sufficient time and funding.

2.   Look for the mathematical or informational principles that a similar environment can do for executing its core principles, and try to run it on the modern computers.

There is a Russian Fairy Tale about Turkish Sultan's Donkey. Sultan had a donkey, which he considered to be a very smart animal, and he wanted to teach him the Turkish language. Sultan sent out an RFP to teach his donkey Turkish language on the following conditions: If within 30 years the donkey will speak the Turkish language, he will award half of the Turkish Kingdom to the applicant. Otherwise, the candidate will be beheaded.

No one applied for the position except one guy. He explained the risk: "In 30 years someone will die. Either me, or Sultan, or his Donkey."

Obviously, author has no intentions to prevent anyone from the option #1 upon such a lousy argument as this fairy tale is. For those, who believe that they may reach a success with option #1 way in a reasonable time, his opinion does not count.

On his side, author simply doesn't think that this approach may be feasible until we have a physical environment that comprises of a hyper huge number of elements behaving exactly like real neurons. But we don't have such environments now, and we don't know when we shall realistically have it.

Author also doesn't think that multiple methods and models developed in the areas of artificial intelligence, cognitive science, neural networks, etc. are wrong and should be tossed for a recreating of some universal model of the brain. In my opinion, accumulated models and methods reflect certain aspects of intelligence.

An Indian Fairy Tale tells us how a few blind people were trying to describe the elephant in the room. One person was touching elephant's tail, another one was touching its trunk, and each one described the elephant differently.

Those blind people are similar to different methods. What is wrong there? The problems started when tail or trunk was presented as the whole elephant. But when we put tail and trunk, and other parts into a coherent system, we will see exactly what the elephant is.

In the same way, we may need to put those different methods into the right places, where they make sense and will work for us. But we also need to find a skeleton for this assembly – a system in which those methods will be functioning properly.

Calvin and Binkerton (2001) in their book *Lingua ex-Machine* provided a funny analogy. Assume that in a distant future, our remote successors dig out a computer from today's world. By that time our existing computer technologies have been lost and become completely forgotten. But their new civilization has also become pretty advanced. And they are using different principles in their information machines, other than binary codes that we are using today.

Our successors somehow managed to start and run the computer, and they see what it can do, but they don't know how. And they decided to study how it works, hoping to get something useful out of it.

As a neuroscientist, Calvin reasonably noticed that the first thing that will happen: our remote successors will try to put probes in the microchips in efforts to understand how this thing works. So this is somewhat similar to what is happening in the Brain Science now.

But this beautiful story can be extended even further. The next thing that will possibly happen: researchers will try to model physical processes with differential equations in the semiconductor junctions. Indeed, such a project will require enormous power, speed, and capacity of their machines, which they expect to reach in tens of years.

So, the goal remains remote. The prevailing opinion is that it is due to the complexity of informational processes in our computer. In a few tens of years, when capacity and performance of their machines will increase exponentially, they expect to reach the level, which may cover a sufficient number of semiconductor junction models.

A group of Ph.D. students studies the theory of binary codes. And they suddenly decide to check where the recently dug out ancient computer may work on the same principles. Voila, their guess is valid. Real informational processes and models are not the same physical processes in the semiconductor junctions, not even close. Binary programming rediscovered, and widely used altogether with newly rebuild digital computers.

It is an excellent analogy about the brain. And possibly, a major lesson is that informational processes may not necessarily be equal to the physical processes in neural hardware. So, the questions are: what are the mathematical models that can describe intelligent processes, and what mathematics can describe them on the level that would be sufficient for practical purposes of modeling?

This book is about cortical math that may help us to avoid building costly environments consisted of models of real neurons. Systematic approach (Meystel & Albus, 2001) looks much more promising. If for instance, we could see that cortical processes can work with graphs or diagrammatic models that could be formalized and programmed.

REFERENCES

Calvin, W., & Binkerton, D. (2001). *Lingua ex-machine*. MIT Press.

Hawkins, J., & Blakeslee, S. (2004). *On intelligence*. St. Martin's Griffin.

Meystel, A. M., & Albus, J. S. (2001). *Intelligent systems: Architecture, design, and control*. New York: Wiley.

Chapter 1
Cognitive Semiotics and the Game of Life

ABSTRACT

This chapter briefly describes overall architectural requirements to the autonomous systems, and provides details on how implicit perceptual symbols emerge in the brain, some evidence from neuroscience, and mathematical methods that can generate implicit symbols from perceptual information.

INTRODUCTION

When we see anything, we neither compute a precise 3-D model of visual scene nor are able to describe in a human language everything that we see. But we can understand what we see. More precisely, we can understand space and time order of what we see, which comprises our visual scene. And we can recognize and name some objects in the visual scene, using our acute foveal vision. And we can understand what we have to do about it. But what does such an "understanding" actually mean?

Neither perception nor cognition processes organize a linear bottom-up sequence. For instance, if you have recognized some objects, this may help you to identify the order of things in the visual scene. And when you have an idea of what kind of visual scene you are observing, it is easier to recognize or identify objects in the visual scene depending on where they are. So, the overall process looks like a filling puzzle.

DOI: 10.4018/978-1-5225-2431-1.ch001

And when we are filling out this puzzle, we are not doing this from scratch every time. In the same way like every other puzzle, this one requires some preliminary knowledge. Without it, solving the problem is not possible.

Solving the problem of vision requires knowledge of the order in the world. We are not able to estimate precisely distances and timings, and this means that no restoration of a precise 3D model ever happens in the brain. But we are always able to say that one object is closer to us than another object. Or, that one event has occurred earlier than another one. And this means that we can understand the relational order of the world that is a subject of a new relational topology.

This order is determined both by physical laws of the world and the ways how human tends to organize information. For instance, human frequently organizes close things into categories and hierarchies.

There is evidence from the cognitive neuroscience that perceptual cortical areas wired in the way that for 1/3 feed-forward projections there are 2/3 backward projections. And this means that some context system does exist and strongly affects human recognition capabilities.

Brain processes information in a hierarchical manner. On the lower levels, we can find perceptual features, and top levels are some cognitive models used for decision making.

The order, in which this puzzle is filled out, may also be crucial for survivability. Some objects or parts of the visual scene may require immediate reaction. But in a general case, visual information is used for planning mostly on tactical and further – on a strategic level. And this conscious or subconscious planning dictates the search order in the visual scene.

Extracted information is used for a tactical decision making and strategic planning. Tactical decision making in a real world is a rapid process because real life rarely gives another chance. And a successful tactical move may not be sufficient if the overall strategy fails on the following steps. So we also need to extract more information for strategic planning. And this is where human hunters were always winning over the animals.

All these processes interact and involve some higher level cognitive knowledge that serves as a context system for recognition. And all of this may help us to solve ambiguity in recognition of real world images. Reliable recognition frequently requires a context, which decreases uncertainty.

Vision is not just about recognition, although recognition is an important part of it. Vision is only a part of a larger system that allows us to build and maintain a reliable model of surrounding environment. And it is a part of situation awareness system that is mandatory for our survival, decision making, planning, and reaching our goals on tactical and strategic levels. And all of this serves as a top-level context system, which significantly affects what we need to search for and recognize in the sensor stream.

People senses have same payload problems that any other information processing system. Certain information has to be identified and processes extremely quickly. Ignoring certain information is safe. Here our context system and senses come into play and effects processing.

And there is another important observation: for solving human problems, we may need a human level of intelligence. Animals are excellent in navigation and moving their bodies in the surrounding world. But would an animal brain even be able to drive a car, it still cannot perform tasks that a real human driver does, because driver's goals and tasks on the route are not just all about driving.

Human level of intellect is needed both for responsible driving and achieving the real goals, which span beyond the driving. A horse cannot be used without its human driver. And when we want a genuinely autonomous system, we need a human level of intellect. Animal's level is insufficient for the practical purposes.

Mind processes were studied since civilization started. But because thought couples tightly with language and logic, such studies were reduced mostly to language and logic until the relatively recent rise of cognitive and information sciences.

Ancient Greeks intensively studied and promoted logical ways of thinking. Logic was appreciated in their disputes and widely used to prove their cases in courts. They also started educating their youth thinking in the same logical ways. Although Aristotle discussed non-logical mechanisms of the mind, this aspect of his theories has been lost, while logical patterns and modes of thought formed the basis of an educational system of Western Civilization. (Perlovsky, 2004)

Giving tribute to the Ancient Greek thinkers, we have a different practical purpose of building intelligent systems, and we will take a look at the problem from that perspective.

Even if we have a well-formalized logic, we are still in the middle of nowhere until we have developed an overall mechanism that could apply this logic in a proper place. (Perlovsky, 2004, 2010)

Same refers to language. There were many efforts to build intelligent system purely upon the language models. These directions followed a simplified understanding of the brain-mind as a logical system, and none of such systems possess necessary qualities that make them work in a human way. Nothing is surprising. The human brain-mind combines language and thinking, but prior systems used language and logic without adequate modeling of language-thinking interaction.

The mind uses context from cognitive and perceptual processes, motor memories, prediction models, etc. And understanding and simulating brain processes requires an understanding of the entire system context.

Another relevant area is emotions. Emotions frequently carry a romantic load and that distorted studies of their real nature. That is correct because they bound tightly with basic instincts of a human. But emotions are also heavily involved in many brain processes, including conscious and unconscious decision making. And this is already a subject of practical interest for building autonomous system.

Just saying all those trivial things does not bring any value. But we will use all these statements above as functional requirements for the system that we want to build.

Such a system should have some mathematical foundation. But it also can be backed by neuroscience. Wherever possible, we will try to demonstrate how brain processes can support those operations.

But methods or APIs may not be per se guarantee any results until they assembled into some working architecture. If we are architecting an autonomous system, we may need to look for some useful analogies if there are any. And there is an analogy in the world of computer games.

We do not mean simple visual toys but advanced games. It is a well knows the fact that such games originated from flight simulators. Later virtual reality added to them a very realistic simulation of the real world. Adding to them some knowledge of the reality and decision making algorithms turned such game software into sophisticated engines that may play against a human.

There is a real game that natural creatures are playing. And this game is called Life. This game may have multiple goals. The primary and most fundamental ones are called instincts. Goals may differ, depending on life conditions. There are many ways to achieve goals, splitting those into sub-processes. And there are sub-goals to execute such processes. If goals cannot be reached, this creates problems. But in any case, a leaving creature will try to reach its goal.

Advanced Computer games have captured some similarities with real life. An example of a virtual reality game engine shown in Figure 1.

What about an autonomous system? It must have a similar driving force, which has world model, is capable of understanding images and video (as

Figure 1. Computer game engine

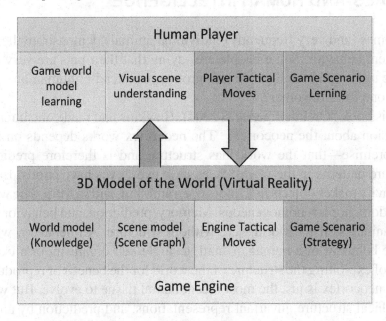

the most informative input stream), does tactical moves in response to the real world information, and plan specific scenario to make tactical moves in particular order to achieve its goals. (See Figure 2)

Figure 2. Autonomous system engine

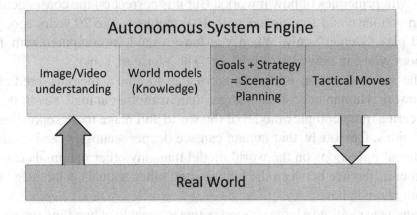

ANIMALS' AND HUMAN INTELLIGENCE

Sometimes (and very frequently) individual animals demonstrate the pretty intelligent behavior. Some people are saying that their pets are very smart. Can we use animal intelligence as a prototype instead of human one? What differs one from the other?

In his book "On Intelligence" (2004), Hawkins had made one interesting conclusion about the neocortex: "The neocortex works depends on a very basic premise—that the world has structure and is therefore predictable. There are patterns in the world: faces have eyes, eyes have pupils, fires are hot, gravity makes objects fall, doors open and shut, and so forth. The world is not random, nor is it homogeneous. Memory, prediction, and behavior would be meaningless if the world were without structure. All behavior, whether it is the behavior of a human, a snail, a single-cell organism, or a tree, is a means of exploiting the structure of the world for the benefit of reproduction.

The neocortex is just the most recent neural tissue to evolve. But with its hierarchical structure, invariant representations, and prediction by analogy, the cortex allows mammals to exploit much more of the structure of the world than an animal without a neocortex can." (Hawkins, 2004, p.180)

Those animals that have no cortex are not able to learn world order and dependencies, don't make any predictions, and just follow their simple instincts. But all mammals have a neocortex. And they are all intelligent, but to differing degrees that their cortex allows them.

There would be an analogy with computer memory. The analogy has nothing to do with principles of how it works. But it is correct on the consequences. When you have had a computer with 16K memory, like 20 years ago, you could play "Digger" only. When you have a modern computer with 16G memory, you can now play "Sims" or "The World of Tanks."

The major function of the neocortex is to run a memory-prediction framework. Human neocortex is larger than in another animal, so our brains can learn a more complex model of the world and make more sophisticated predictions. Obviously, that human can see deeper analogies, and do more intelligent operations on the world model than any other mammals can do. Another difference between the humans and other animals is language that the only human have.

Language required a large neocortex that is capable of handling the nested structures of syntax and semantics. Language is a mean of communication between individuals, and it can both transmit to and receive from other human learned patterns. So our neocortex may learn new structures and relations from the language, using the experience of another person. Animals can't transmit as much information to their species.

Everything in a human brain exists in a reptile's and a mammal's brains but a large cortex. The vast area of human neocortex is what makes humans smarter than any other mammals. But the human cortex builds with a commonly repeated element of the same thickness and nearly the same structure as the cortex in orther mammals. (Hwakins, 2004)

Human got smart by adding more elements of a common cortical algorithm. Interestingly, but many researchers mentioned that the neocortex increase in human is not a product of a slow evolution but rather looks like a rapid upgrade on the time scale. And computer memory upgrade from 32K to 16G which brought more processing capacity would be a valid analogy, although computational algorithms of the computer and cortex are drastically different.

Mammals with neocortex were able to recall more which behaviors led them to needed goals, and in that way predict the future more intelligently about what will happen next. An animal without a neocortex has a much poorer ability to remember the past, and it may start from scratch in the same situation every time. Mammals understand the world and their nearest future because of their cortical memory.

By comparing the actual sensory input with recalled memory, the animal not only knows where it is, but it can predict the future. So animals can move more efficiently through the world because they can predict the future. A human could form more memories, and make more predictions. The complexity of the memories and predictions also increased.

But human brains are also connected up differently from animals. The word "anterior" is used for the front half and the word "posterior" for the back half of the cortex. Sensory perception primarily occurs in the posterior regions of the cortex. Anterior regions of cortex that are involved in high-level planning and thought. It also contains the motor cortex, and it is responsible for creating behavior.

Human has a vast anterior cortex, and human motor cortex makes many more connections with the body muscles than other mammals do.

Hawkins (2004) nicely described this situation: "…adding a memory system and feeding the sensory stream into it, the animal could remember past experiences. When the animal found itself in the same or a similar situation, the memory would be recalled, leading to a prediction of what was likely to happen next. Thus, intelligence and understanding started as a memory system that fed predictions into the sensory stream. These predictions are

7

the essence of understanding. To know something means that you can make predictions about it.

The cortex evolved in two directions. First, it got larger and more sophisticated in the types of memories it could store; it was able to remember more things and make predictions based on more complex relationships. Second, it started interacting with the motor system of the old brain. To predict what you will hear, see, and feel next, it needed to know what actions were taken. With humans, the cortex has taken over most of our motor behavior. Instead of just making predictions based on the behavior of the old brain, the human neocortex directs behavior to satisfy its predictions." (Hawkins, 2004, p.104)

And here comes the obvious. For the solution of human tasks, the intellect of autonomous system must be at least at the human level. No one has ever seen an animal driving a car. Even the most intelligent animals like chimpanzee have no capabilities to be trained for that.

CORTICAL FUNCTIONS

Although brain and neural system were studied intensively, some phenomena, like Hebbian learning, have attracted significant attention, while some others remained outliers. However, it is already obvious that creative informational processes like mind exist on the cortical level rather than on the level of individual neurons. And cortex is organized in the complex multilevel hierarchical structure of layered neural assemblies.

Significant neuroscience research intensively studied cortex. It appeared that different cortical areas are responsible for different functions. Researchers had tried to find the physiological distinctions between the regions. But it appeared that different cortical regions look on the physiological pretty much the same.

Dr. V. Mountcastle, "The Father of Neuroscience," had shown that despite the functional differences, the neocortex is uniform on the physiological level. The same six layers, same cell types, and same connectivity are in every functional cortical region. (Mountcastle, 1978)

His natural conclusion was that cortex is practically homogeneous in its physiology. And this means that the same type of computations and informational processes happen everywhere in the cortex, independently of the functional region. Different is the processing data, and where the region is getting feeds from other regions and other parts of nervous system.

Mountcastle (1978) concluded that there is standard functionality in all the cortical regions, and the cortical tissue itself is doing the same thing everywhere.

Someone may suggest: Okay, let's model physical processes in that cortical organization, and eventually we may understand how the mind works. This approach may give some results. But it is hard to figure out what is going on without any hypothetical understanding of how intelligent operations may happen.

One of the most important observations in the neuroscience was that information is processing in the brain in a particular hierarchy of functional regions. But the hierarchy has nothing to do with their physical arrangement in the brain.

All the functional areas of the cortex reside in the same cortical sheet. Lower areas send information up; higher areas send feedback information down to lower areas. There are also lateral connections between areas (See Figures 3, 4).

Sensory information first arrives into the primary sensory areas. Visual information enters the primary visual area V1, which reacts on low-level visual features such as color contrast, edges, small motion, and binocular disparity.

V1 feeds information up to areas V2, V4, and IT (also known as TE). V4 respond to some objects of medium complexity, Area IT responds to objects like animals, faces, etc. (See Figure 5)

Area MT responds the motions of objects. Sensory information from different senses passes into "association areas."

Descriptions of brain processes are a simplistic view of hierarchies. Information enters the primary sensory areas, and outcomes move up the hierarchy, gets passed through the association areas, and then to the frontal lobes of the cortex, and finally, gets passed back down to the motor areas.

Per Hawkins (2004), this view is completely wrong. Because information in the cortex also flows in the opposite direction, with many more projections feeding back down the hierarchy than up. Higher regions of the cortex send more signals "down" to primary visual cortex than it gets from the eye.

The wiring of the neocortex can change and rewire itself depending on the type of inputs flowing into it. This means that V. Mountcastle ideas are correct, and neither cortical cells are physically specialized for particular kind of information, nor cortex is rigidly designed to perform different functions.

Figure 3. Revealed interconnections of some cortical areas and subcortical structures related to the perceptual processing of visual information. Double arrows denote both forward and feedback projections. Interpretation of functions of some cortical areas is still controversial and has to be refined. All researchers consistently reported the existence of different pathways of visual processing information. Such pathways are known in the literature as "What" (also known as Ventral or Temporal) and "Where" or "How" (also known as Dorsal or Parietal). Pathways are interconnected, and the modular separation of areas is a simplification. This entire system looks rather as a distributed graph, where different paths are responsible for the processing of different information.

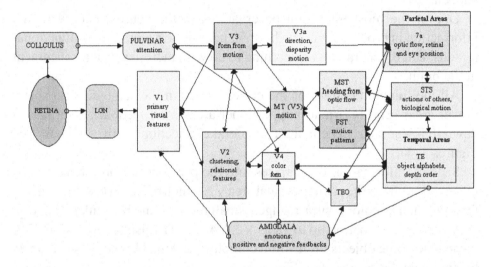

Figure 4. A general schema of perception (adopted from Kosslyn, 1996). The "where" (dorsal) pathway is a spatial-features encoding system, whereas the "what" (ventral) pathway, is an object-features encoding subsystem. Outputs from both pathways come together in an "associative memory" in the prefrontal areas. Recognition occurs when an input matches a memory in the "what" system. Identification takes place when input image matches a stored representation in the associative memory.

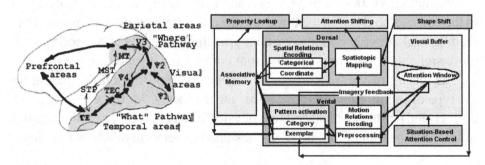

Figure 5. Schematic description of reactions observed in the cortical area IT (adopted from Tanaka, 1996)

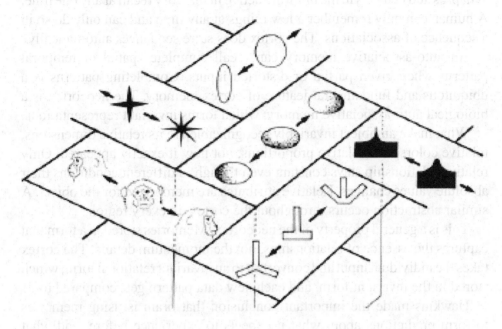

Rather, brain regions develop specialized functions for the information that flows into them. Signals from different senses are different, but in the cortex, they turn into the patterns of cells activities and are all handled in similar ways by the cortical layers. There is no fundamental difference between these types of information. The brain only knows patterns of action potentials in particular places or areas of the cortex. Both perceptions and world knowledge are built from those patterns. (Hawkins, 2004).

Vision carries both spatial and temporal information. The patterns sent into the brain are completely changing with eye saccade. And brains are machines for processing cortical patterns.

J. Hawkins (2004) suggested the following functionality in the neocortex:

- The neocortex stores sequences of patterns.
- The neocortex recalls patterns auto-associatively.
- The neocortex stores patterns in an invariant form.
- The neocortex stores patterns in a hierarchy.

Despite an enormous potential storing capacity, only a limited number of synapses and neurons in the brain are active in memory recall at any one time. A human can only remember a few things at any time and can only do so in a sequence of associations. The cortex does store sequences automatically.

An auto-associative memory can recall complete spatial or temporal patterns when given partial or distorted inputs. Completing patterns is a ubiquitous and fundamental feature of cortex memory. The neocortex is a biological auto-associative memory, which forms invariant representations.

What make an object invariably recognizable are its relative dimensions, relative colors, and relative proportions, not how it exactly appeared. Only relative relationship stays constant even though in different conditions their absolute values changes. Relative attributes are memorized for the object. A similar abstraction occurs throughout the cortex, in every region.

This is a general property of the neocortex. Memories stored in a form that captures the essence of relationships, not the momentum details. The cortex takes the individual input and converts it to an invariant relational form, which stored in the invariant form, and each new data pattern gets compared to it.

Hawkins made the important conclusion that brain is using memories to form predictions about what it expects to experience before, and what we perceive is a combination of what we sense and of our brains' memory-derived predictions.

"Brain makes low-level sensory predictions about what it expects to see, hear, and feel at every given moment, and it does so in parallel. All regions of your neocortex are simultaneously trying to predict what their next experience will be. Visual areas make predictions about edges, shapes, objects, locations, and motions. Auditory areas make predictions about tones, direction to the source, and patterns of sound. Somatosensory areas make predictions about touch, texture, contour, and temperature.

"Prediction" means that the neurons involved in sensing become active in advance of them receiving sensory input. When the sensory input does arrive, it is compared with what was expected. Cortex is forming a slew of predictions based on experience.

When all predictions are met, you'll walk through the door without consciously knowing these predictions were verified. But if your expectations about the door are violated, the error will cause you to take notice. Correct predictions result in understanding. The door is normal. Incorrect predictions result in confusion and prompt you to pay attention.

Prediction is the primary function of the neocortex and the foundation of intelligence. The cortex is an organ of prediction. If we want to understand what intelligence is, what creativity is, how your brain works, and how to build intelligent machines, we must understand the nature of these predictions and how the cortex makes them. Even behavior is best understood as a by-product of prediction. (Hawkins, 2004, p. 89)

Despite efforts of many others world-famous scientists like for instance Mumford at Brown, Rao at the UW, Grossberg at BU, have written and theorized about the role of feedback and prediction in various ways, we should give Hawkins a big credit for putting these disparate pieces into a coherent theoretical framework.

Cortex fills in memories of similar patterns for any missing input with what it thinks should be there to perceive an unambiguous image. Attention is immediately aroused when the prediction is violated.

The human brain can make predictions about more abstract patterns and longer sequences than animal brain can. Higher intelligence is not different from perceptual intelligence. According to Mountcastle (1978), it rests on the same neocortical memory and prediction algorithms. The brain receives inputs from the world, stores them in memories, and makes predictions, combining what it was before and what it is now.

INVARIANT REPRESENTATIONS IN THE CORTEX

The joint activity on a bundle of neuronal fibers is what is meant by the pattern. The pattern arriving at V1 can be spatial and temporal.

Receptive field of each V1 neuron is bound to a part of total field of vision. Each V1 cell tuned for particular kinds of such input patterns. Cells in the area IT activate when entire objects, like a human face, appear in the visual field. The transformation from fast to slow changing and from spatially specific to invariant well documented in the research reports.

Information also flows from higher to lower regions via a network of feedback connections from higher areas like IT to lower areas like V4, V2, and V1. Moreover, feedback connections in visual cortex usually exceed feedforward connections.

The same feedforward-feedback process is occurring in all cortical areas involving all senses. This process is needed for prediction to compare to what is happening and what is expected to happen.

Realistically, all cortical regions are collections of many smaller sub-regions/areas. The job of any such area is to find out how its inputs are related, to memorize the sequence of correlations between them, and to use this memory to predict how the data will behave in the future. This cortical process creates invariant relational representations.

Per Hawkins (2004) model, the invariant representations form in every cortical region. Invariance doesn't magically appear in IT. Every region forms invariant representations from the input areas hierarchically below it. Thus all areas of cortex form invariant representations of the world underneath them in the hierarchy.

One of the most important concepts in his book is that the cortex's hierarchical structure stores a model of the hierarchical structure of the real world. Or, the real world's nested structure is mirrored by the nested structure of the cortex.

All objects in your world are composed of subobjects that occur consistently together; that is the very definition of an object. When we assign a name to something, we do so because a set of features consistently travels together. A face is a face precisely because two eyes, a nose, and a mouth always appear together.

Every object in the world is composed of a collection of smaller objects, and most objects are part of larger objects. This is what I mean by nested structure. Once you are aware of it, you can see nested structures everywhere. In an exactly analogous way, your memories of things and the way your brain represents them are stored in the hierarchical structure of the cortex.

Your memory of your home does not exist in one region of cortex. It is stored in a hierarchy of cortical regions that reflect the hierarchical structure of the home. Large-scale relationships are stored at the top of the hierarchy, and small-scale relationships are stored toward the bottom.

The design of the cortex and the method by which it learns naturally discover the hierarchical relationships in the world. (Hawkins, 2004, p. 75)

Per Hawkins, the cortex has a smart learning algorithm that usually finds whatever hierarchical structure exists and captures it. And in the absence of the structure human feel a confusion.

Since a human can only sense a small part of the world at any moment in time, information arrives into the brain as a sequence of patterns. The cortex learns repeated sequences. They are stable and therefore repeated.

A sequence is a set of patterns that accompany each other in time, even if not in a particular fixed order. They are statistically related and tend to occur together in time, although the order may vary.

Each region of cortex receives such patterns in a stream. If the patterns repeated, the area can learn this sequence to predict next pattern. In this way, the cortical region memorizes the sequence. Sequences of patterns are forming invariant representations of the real-world objects.

Abstract and concrete objects are treated in the same way just as sequences of patterns that occur together over time in a predictable fashion. The reliable predictability is a way of knowing that different events in the world are physically tied together.

According to Hawkins (2004), the brain can store sequences of sequences. Each region of the cortex learns sequences, develops "names" for the sequences it knows and passes these names to the next areas higher in the cortical hierarchy.

As information moves up from primary sensory regions to higher levels, there are fewer and fewer changes over time. In V1, the set of active cells is changing rapidly as new patterns fall on the retina. In the IT cell firing patterns are more stable.

The important conclusion Hawkins (2004) had made about naming a sequence of patterns:

Each cortical region has a "name" for each sequence it knows. This "name" is a group of cells whose collective firing represents the set of objects in the sequence. These cells remain active as long as the sequence is playing, and it is this "name" that is passed up to the next region in the hierarchy. As long as the input patterns are part of a predictable sequence, the region presents a constant "name" to the next higher region.

It's as if the region were saying, "Here is the name of the sequence that I am hearing, seeing, or touching. You don't need to know about the individual notes, edges, or texture. I will let you know if something new or unpredicted happens."

More specifically, we can imagine region IT at the top of the visual hierarchy relating to an association area above it, "I see a face. Yes, with each saccade the eyes are fixating on different parts of the face; I see different parts of the face in succession. But it is still the same face. I will let you know when I see something else." In this fashion, a predictable sequence of events gets identified with a "name"—a constant pattern of cell firing."

This happens on every level of the hierarchical pyramid. When collapsing predictable sequences into "named objects" at each region in the hierarchy, more stability is achieved on the higher level. This creates invariant representations. When a pattern moves back down the hierarchy, it gets "unfolded" into sequences.

The unfolding of sequences occurs in the sensory to perceive and understand objects from different views.

When something goes wrong, then the issue arises the hierarchy until someone knows what to do next. When not anticipated patterns occur, information about them progresses up the cortical hierarchy until some region can handle it.

A region first classifies its inputs as a limited number of possibilities and then looks for sequences. "Imagine that you are a single cortical region. Your task is to sort colored pieces of paper. You are supplied ten buckets, each of which is labeled with a sample color swatch. There is one bucket for green, one for yellow, another for red, and so on. You are then given pieces of colored paper, one by one, and told to sort them by color. Each paper you receive is slightly different. Because there are an infinite number of colors in the world, you never get two pieces of paper with the same color. Sometimes it is easy to say what bucket the colored paper should be placed in, but sometimes it is difficult. A paper that is halfway between red and orange could go in either bucket, but you have to assign it to one bucket, either red or orange, even if the selection comes down to a random pick.

A region of cortex not only learns familiar sequences, but it also learns how to modify its classifications. Now the buckets better fit what you see; you have reduced the ambiguity. The cortex is flexible. (Hawkins, 2004, p. 136)

Both classification and sequence formation are necessary to create invariant representations, and each region of cortex does them. This also works as a context system.

Most of the times human are filling in ambiguous or incomplete information from your memories of sequences, hearing what they expect to hear and see what they expect to see when it fits into the experience.

The memory of sequences allows to resolve ambiguity in the current input and to predict which information should happen next. A recognized sequence of patterns helps the cortical region to predict its next data pattern, and tells below region what to expect.

Per Hawkins: "Unlike a camera's memory, the human brain remembers the world as it is, not as it appears. When human think about the world, they are recalling sequences of patterns that correspond to the way the objects in the world are and how they behave, but not how they appear through any particular sense at any point in time. The sequences by which human experience objects in the world reflect the invariant structure of the world itself. The order in which you experience parts of the world is determined by the world's structure. The sequences by which you experience the world is the real structure of the world, and that is what the cortex wants to remember." (Hawkins, 2004, p.137)

Hawkins and his colleagues proposed model of auto-associative memory that they call Hierarchical Temporal Memory (HTM), which is shown below in the Figure 6. Unlike a regular multilevel hierarchical neural networks, the HTM model has multiple feedback connections between nodes of the neighbor levels.

Figure 7 shows activation spreading in the HTM. When a set of nodes on some level are activated by a particular pattern or sequence, activation spreads to the top levels as in the conventional multilevel neural networks. But nodes on the current level also may receive additional activation from the top level nodes. The HTM is supposed to auto-balance and memorize and recognize certain sequences of patterns.

More detailed description of HTM goes beyond this book, and can be found on the Dr. Hawkins Company's "Numenta" website www.numenta.com.

Figure 6. Simplified model of hierarchical temporal memory (HTM) by J. Hawkins

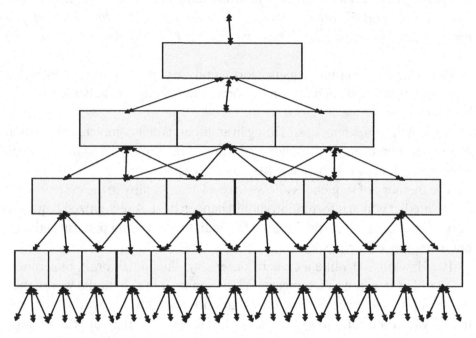

Figure 7. Activation spreading in HTM. Light rectangles didn't receive any activation, dark rectangles directly activated by the input pattern. Existence of feedback may cause additional activation processes in the HTM from the top.

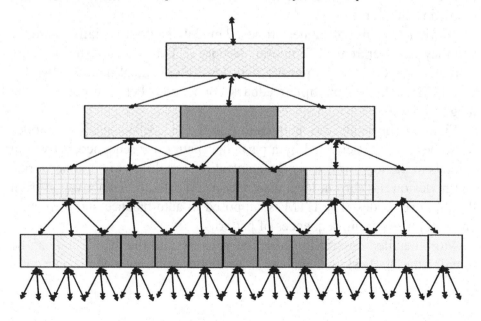

CORTICAL COLUMN AS A TYPICAL PROCESSING UNIT

The physiological processing unit in the neocortex is a so-called column, discovered by Hubel and Wessel (2004). The human cortex has an estimated several hundred million micro-columns. (See Figure 8)

Mountcastle proposed that the cortical column is the core unit of computation in the cortex. J. Hawkin believes that a column is the core unit of prediction. On my side, I think that cortical column may play different roles in different cortical areas.

Per Hawkins (2004), converging patterns going up the cortical hierarchy, diverging patterns going down the cortical hierarchy, and a delayed feedback through the thalamus. A region of cortex classifies its inputs, learns sequences of patterns, forms a consistent pattern or "name" for a sequence, and makes accurate predictions.

The columns in a region of cortex provide a set of unique values for classifying our inputs. The output of each column represents the label for a chosen value. Inputs from the lower level are connected to the layer IV cells in every column. A column with strongest input prevents other columns from firing.

Figure 8. Cortical column (adopted from Hubel and Wessel, 2004)

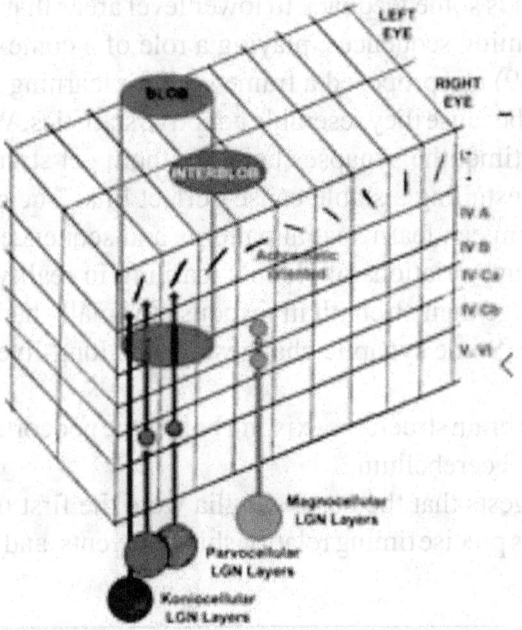

This is achieved with inhibitory cells. This mechanism is known as Winner-Takes-All, or System of Inhibition and Excitation. This allows for producing the unambiguous answer. Famous Russian Neuroscientist N. Amosov called this "A System of Activations and Inhibitions."

When a column becomes active multiple times, it sends output to higher regions. But there are also back projections. Once an output is sent again, column gets an anticipation signals back, helping to recognize anticipated pattern.

A column also receives excitatory connections from the similar neighbor columns. That helps in processing lines of a certain orientation that cover. Similar mechanisms are observed for higher cortical areas, although for more complex patterns.

Interestingly that in addition to projecting to lower cortical regions, a lowest layer VI cells of column can send their output back into the layer IV cells of their column. S. Grossberg calls this "folded feedback," (1987) while in Hawkins terminology (2004) this is called "imagining."

The connections in the cortical hierarchy are reciprocal. There are often more axons going backward than forward. It seems wrong to say that most of the thousands of synapses on a neuron play only a modulatory role. Massive feedback with huge numbers of synapses exists for a reason.

Summarizing: In Hawkins (2004) terminology, cortical columns send the implicit name of the sequence into higher regions in response to an input sequence and sends some feedback to lower level areas that allow to fine turn or filter the incoming sequences, playing a role of a context system.

D. Hebb (1949) has proposed a framework for learning, and his ideas are widely accepted because they resemble adaptive statistics. When two neurons fire at the same time, the synapses between them get strengthened. This is also a basis for installing a stable cause –effect link. The classical Hebbian learning algorithm can learn spatial patterns and sequences of patterns.

There are many variations of Hebb's learning in reality. Some synapses may rapidly change their strength in response to small changes in the timing of neural signals. Some synaptic changes may be long-lived, other ones are short-lived.

They are three brain structures existing before the neocortex: hippocampus, basal ganglia, and cerebellum.

Hawkins suggests that the basal ganglia were the first motor system, the cerebellum learns precise timing relationships of events, and the hippocampus stored memories of specific events and places. Later the neocortex has subsumed their original functions at least partially. For instance, the neocortex is responsible for complex motor sequences.

The hippocampus is essential to the formation of new memories. People, who lost the hippocampus lost the ability to form most new memories. Everything that was learned before that loss appears normal.

A second major parallel pathway for passing information from region to region, up the hierarchy goes through layer 5 of cortical columns to the thalamus, and the thalamus sends connections up to the next higher region of cortex. If two regions of cortex connect to each other in a hierarchy, there is also a forward connection through the thalamus.

Hawkins speculates that the alternate pathway through the thalamus is the mechanism by which we attend to details that usually we wouldn't notice. It bypasses the grouping of sequences in layer 2, sending the raw data to the next higher region of cortex.

Researchers have shown that the alternate pathway can be turned on either by a particular request signal from the higher region of the cortex itself or by a substantial unexpected signal from below. If the input to the alternate pathway is active enough, it sends a wake-up signal to the higher region, which again can turn on the path.

Per Hawkins (2004), creativity is an inherent property of every cortical region, and it is a necessary component of prediction. Our invariant memories are of sequences of events. We make predictions by combining the invariant memory recall of what should happen next with the details about this moment in time. Prediction is the application of invariant memory sequences to the new situations.

Therefore all cortical predictions are predictions by analogy. And this goes unnoticeable. When the memory-prediction system operates at a higher level of abstraction, only then it makes uncommon predictions, using uncommon analogies. They create unexpected analogies as a means of teaching higher-level structure.

Let's match what we have learned from the previous chapter against the abstract informational models and patterns accumulated by the Computer and Informational Sciences. Our goal is to emulate intelligent systems and algorithms using information from the brain and cognitive studies; therefore this exercise makes a lot of sense.

One of the first analogies that come to mind is related to memory usage in stateful and stateless processes. The stateless process depends only on its inputs, while stateful process depends on its data and its memory. Memory is something, where the process can write. Otherwise, it is simply another input.

Another pattern is an operational and permanent memory. The process can use an operational memory, even accumulate some data, and use it for decisions points. But once the process is over, the cumulative memory is lost. And next time the process starts from scratch again.

Life is a set of situations that require a fast reaction. And in the most cases, it doesn't give another chance to replay. So, neither stateless nor stateful algorithms without permanent memory are very helpful in surviving. Simplest organisms, which behave in such a way, may not have a high survival rate. If such species still exist in nature, this can be attributed rather to their enormous fertility.

Obviously, this is not the case for the human brain. The operational and permanent memory may be called short-term and long-term memory. Although physical memory mechanisms in the biological and computer systems are different, the processes that accumulate previous experience from the past runs, and use this knowledge for prediction later, can be easily done within the existing computer paradigm.

Hawkins book (2004) describes a hierarchically organized sequence memory, where past accumulated patterns are used for prediction of the current ones.

No one would possibly disagree with that picture of informational cortical processes as above. A top level sequence node recognizes sequences from the lower level nodes. More levels we have more complex sequences we can remember, and smarter we are. Is there anything lacking in such a beautiful model of intelligence?

But this a typical reactive model based on the paradigm of Recognition – Action. Following this model, we see, and we react. We see a banana in our visual sequence. And we grab it and eat with a motor sequence when we are hungry. Etc.

Ouch, someone just painfully hit us for stealing, when we grabbed a banana. And through the pain, we learned not to grab anything immediately just when we see it. But rather do some other sequences that are not leading to the pain. And we are growing our intelligence in this very same way, up until our IQ has risen to the level of Einstein.

Sorry, but this is not how we human are getting smart. Purely reactive behavior is a common animals' behavior, whose intellectual capabilities are very weak. Animals' behavior has been studied as intensively as humans' one, and this is how animals behave all their lives.

A human may use this behavioral pattern as dominant in the very early childhood. But no one may call it "intelligence." And in a no way, our intelligence may grow up to the Einstein level in this way.

Yes, something important is missing. There must be some mechanisms that make us significantly different from animals. Our intellectual ability to appropriately interact in society, our ability to develop abstract mental models and build plans, our ability to learn abstract ideas from language and visual constructs, our ability to generate advanced algorithms that help us in reaching our goals, our ability to make analogies, our ability to create things upon mental models, our logical capabilities, etc. This list can be endless.

The major point here is that all those capabilities just may not be explained with a pure "learning – recall" process. So we may need to find mechanisms that can provide such phenomena. Some higher animals like Bonobo may demonstrate certain intelligent capabilities to some child degree. But that only means that they also have such mechanisms, although much less sophisticated than human's ones.

A major problem in discovering mechanisms that are responsible for intelligence is that it is very similar to the imaginary case of re-discovering of a digital computer, described before. While physical processes are visible, informational processes may be entirely different from the physical processes. Another word, we need to know what to look for.

But how can we know what to look for? During the past decade's scientists were intensively trying to model the cognitive processes, and they have accumulated multiple abstract models. The biggest problem with such models always was that each model was able to cover only certain aspects of cognition, but was positioned by media as a universal solution for all cognitive problems.

It would be wrong to ignore such models, saying that they are not adequate. We rather may need to look how to combine such models and methods into a universal system that can also be backed up with results of cognitive and neural sciences. Also, such a system should be able to explain gestalts and other cognitive phenomena, which were found by cognate science but didn't find an explanation regarding existing models.

DECISIONS, CERTAINTY, AND THEIR TOPOLOGICAL MODEL

All neurons cell body has branching axons and dendrites. Axons connect to the dendrites of another with synapses. The nerve impulse from the cell influences the behavior of other cells via its synapses. Synapses can be inhibitory or excitatory. Spiking neural signal at a synapse creates conditions for the recipient cell to a spike in excitatory synapses. Inhibitory synapses decrease the recipient cell ability to spike.

There is interesting phenomenon observed. The strength of a synapse varies in time, depending on the history. For the excitatory synapses, change is that when two neurons generate a spike at nearly the same time, the connection strength between the two neurons will be increased.

Author will say more about this process, called Hebbian learning (1949), a bit later. Not only a synapse is changing the strength, but entirely new synapses can form between the neurons. It may be happening all the time, although the scientific evidence is controversial. Regardless of the details of how synapses change their strength, what is certain is that the formation and strengthening of synapses are what causes memories to be stored.

A human neocortex typically contains around thirty billion neurons. Anyway, our learning capabilities are very limited. An average person learns around 5 thousand words of human language. A more exceptional individual may know around 10 thousand. Just this simple fact has already demonstrated that a single neuron is insufficient for memorizing concepts. This is a neural assembly that matters. Cortical neurons connected into functional modules conceived as a column. The entire neocortex consists of this structure.

Neurons in a particular cortical location may oscillate in response to a certain pattern. On the physical level activated cells oscillate at a distinctive higher frequency. This phenomenon is called resonance in different sources.

Informational representation of resonance is a bell-shaped or trapezoidal filter function (See Figure 9). The integrative pattern of cortical activity can be represented the same way. Y. Burnod (1991) showed that the spatiotemporal pattern of cortical activities could be modeled with trapezoidal temporal forms (p.80), which is the form of a fuzzy set. And Burnod is not the only one who independently came to this idea. (See Figure 9)

Hebbian learning in neurons is a very important phenomenon. It proved that neural assemblies are capable of doing adaptive statistics. But this

Figure 9. Informational representations of resonance are bell-shaped functions (left). The introduction of Certainty Dimension or normalization converts such a function into a fuzzy set (center). The core of such fuzzy set is 100% certain and can represent a point in a qualitative graph model (right), or an implicit symbol in a symbolic system.

phenomenon may only explain some learning, and it not able to explain higher order processes such as mind.

So we may need to leave aside the Hebbian learning, and look for other phenomena.

One of such phenomena is so-called resonance. Neurons in a particular cortical location may oscillate in response to a certain pattern. However, that also led to the situation when activation of a certain group of neurons also inhibits surrounding neurons, which could be possibly activated by a significantly different pattern. This phenomenon is so important that great Soviet Neuroscientist Amosov even called it as a System of Activation-Inhibition.

The system works as a set of resonance filters, each response to a particular stimulus pattern. However, only one of them can be selected with certainty, which is similar to a quantization of continuous scale by the set of discrete values. The same mechanism of the linguistic variable was proposed by Lotfi Zadeh (1975).

The idea of linguistic variable is shown in Figure 10.

Hawkins analyzes the problem of combinational complexity that arises from the fact that input patterns are carried on thousands or millions of axons. The number of possible patterns that can exist on even one thousand axons is larger than the number of molecules in the universe. So when a single region stores sequences, what are they sequences of?

Hawkins suggests that a cortex region first classifies its inputs as one of a limited number of possibilities, and then looks for sequences. If we grade color, we may reduce it to a few limited names similar to what we human do with color scale.

The color that is halfway between red and orange could go in either name, but only one, either red or orange, even if the selection comes down

Figure 10. Quantification of a real axis with a set of bell-shaped resonance filters (left). The introduction of Certainty Dimension or normalization converts them into fuzzy sets (right). The dual structure on the right is a Symbolic Space, combining quantitative continuous and qualitative discrete parts. Such structure emulates the set of filters or feature detectors. But in the Certainty Dimension, it is also equivalent to a set of unique points that is similar to the set of implicit symbols of an alphabet. Learning in a distributed, continuous environment is the process of dynamic creation of transfer function that maps input to the desired output. That means that we can create new and modify old such symbols "on the fly."

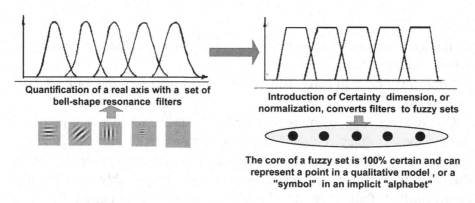

Quantification of a real axis with a set of bell-shape resonance filters

Introduction of Certainty dimension, or normalization, converts filters to fuzzy sets

The core of a fuzzy set is 100% certain and can represent a point in a qualitative model , or a "symbol" in an implicit "alphabet"

to a random pick. Such an ambiguity also can be resolved with the help of top-down context.

We should mention here that such operations are equivalent to Linguistic Variable introduced by L.Zadeh (1975) Linguistic Variable allows quantifying a quantitative scale into a set of discrete qualitative values.(See Figure 11)

The quantification of color scale is purely subjective. Different cultures have different sets of colors in their languages. A system equipped with such a structure really "understand" different colors. The implicit symbolic values of color from the Color Device can be used for decisions and logical operations.

We have a dual structure where input values correspond to a distinctive name. This name is a qualitative value, and it can stand on a higher level as a single entity for the input values, which it represents. Such operations conform to the basic principles of Semiotics. What Hawkins calls "name" is called there a "symbol" that can stand for a recognized pattern. The pattern may denote a property, object, relation, sequence, or any entity.

Humans can understand different aspects of visual information: color, sizes, ranges, distances without accurate computations. Solving the mystery, we have to introduce the concept of "measuring device." Such device is a

Figure 11. Quantization of color scale with Linguistic Variable. The scale of light waves is quantified by fuzzy sets of rainbow colors. Certainty dimension turns the continuous scale into a set of discrete linguistic values – an alphabet of colors. The point in the qualitative part represents a symbol of color. A color does not require explicit naming. A reference, or link, to the appropriate point, is used instead. This way our system can "understand" a core set of 7 colors, and use them in logical operations. If the system needs more gradations of color for logical operations, it can be done the same way. Color naming is subjective, and different cultures quantified color scale differently from the currently accepted Western set of 7 primary colors. But the element of a set must not necessarily have a linguistic value. Regarding semiotic, the element of the set means a symbol, which denotes a particular pattern or a feature, whatever mechanism may produce such symbols and their alphabets.

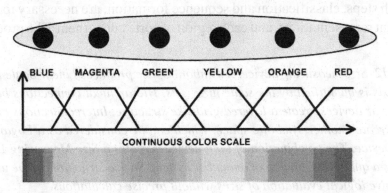

dual derivative structure that is used for evaluation. The examples are Color Device and Size Measuring Device on Figures 11-12.

The Color Device is composed of the set of fuzzy filters. This is a natural way of how humans make concepts of colors. Such quantification is subjective, and different cultures had different sets of colors in their languages. Anyway, a system equipped with such structure really "understand" different colors. The values of color can be used for decisions and logical operations.

There is evidence that something similar exists in the cortical area V4. Destruction of that cortical area makes people color blind. Some researchers say that such damage destructs the ability to separate colors. We know about Self-Organizing Maps in the brain, and that such maps create symbolic spaces. Therefore, a loss of V4 can destroy such "device." The ability "to understand" colors is gone, which means a color blindness.

Understanding of sizes and proportions also requires a qualitative structure. A single layer represents a Linear Scale Device -- a symbolic space, where each symbol corresponds to the same range. Logarithmic Scale Device is another symbolic space where each symbol denotes a different layer. Their combination creates a Size Measuring Device, able to evaluate dimensions and proportions qualitatively. There is a strong analogy between such device and a number system. Also, visual receptive fields are similarly hierarchically connected in the optic tract.

Scales, lattices and other kinds of similar devices, build upon secondary structures, give the opportunity to analyze and verify. Unlike a hard-coded program, such structures provide more flexible mechanisms. They can be both algorithms and data at the same time. Another algorithm can use them as data.

Both steps, classification and sequence formation, are necessary to create invariant representations, and each region of cortex does them. The process of

Figure 12. Size measuring device. A symbolic space produces Linear Scale Device if the axis is quantified by the same fuzzy sets. Hierarchical connections between such linear devices create a layered grid-like structure. Interconnections between layers create another symbolic space, which can be considered as a Logarithmic Scale Device. The combination of both devices creates a Size Measuring Device, which is a qualitative analog of a number system. Such a structure can be used for qualitative logical evaluation of sizes without precise calculations.

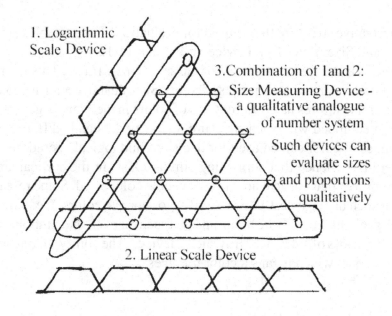

1. Logarithmic Scale Device

3. Combination of 1 and 2: Size Measuring Device - a qualitative analogue of number system

Such devices can evaluate sizes and proportions qualitatively

2. Linear Scale Device

forming sequences pays off when an input is ambiguous, and the context of known sequences is used to resolve the ambiguity. The memory of sequences allows not only to resolve ambiguity in the current input but also to predict which information should happen next. A pattern moves back down the hierarchy: stable patterns get "unfolded" into sequences.

In cortical regions, bottom-up classifications and top-down sequences are constantly interacting, changing throughout the life. This is the essence of learning.

Primary visual areas convert visual information into a "granular" symbolic form. Objects and other stable systems have coherent relational structures. Hierarchical compression and other transformations in the higher cortical areas derive more abstract structures, which makes possible the recognition of a particular structure as an exemplary of a class.

The initial quantization of visual information happens first on the receptive field of the retina. The quantized information travels from retina to the LGN and then to the primary visual area, V1. The receptive fields of the LGN can process more sophisticated features than retinal receptive fields. Similar to the retina and the LGN, V1 is a retinotopic area. There is evidence that primary area V1 plays the role of a "visual buffer" for the human brain.

Hubel and Weisel (2004) found that the information processing structure of V1 is organized into hypercolumns. A hypercolumn is a kind of supermodule that covers all features of a particular retinal point and consists of alternating columns for each eye. The orientation sensitivity of the columns includes all possible angles within a retinal area. So-called blobs – neural clusters that are responsible for the processing of color information -- are discontinuities within the hypercolumns. (See Figure 8).

Regarding Semiotic systems, a hypercolumn can be represented by a set of symbolic spaces for color, orientation, and disparity that are bounded to a particular retinal point or small local area. In this sense, a hypercolumn is considered to be a very complex receptive field that is capable of working with vectors or spaces of features or symbols that can be derived from a particular point or a small local neighborhood area of an image.

Representations of images as cognitive semiotic structures solve the mysterious image understanding problems. Humans understand color, size, distance, and other properties without accurate computations. And cognitive semiotic structure could play the role of a "measuring device."

The Color Device is a Symbolic Space composed of a set of fuzzy filters upon the color scale. The range of light waves is quantified by fuzzy sets of rainbow colors. The point in the qualitative part represents an implicit

29

symbol of color. In this representation, the color does not require explicit naming. A reference, or link, to the appropriate point, is used instead. In this way, the system can "understand" a basic set of colors and use them in logical operations. If the system needs more gradations of color for logical operations, this can be done in the same way.

The Orientation Device (See Figure 13) is another symbolic space that quantifies the scale of orientation angles by the use of fuzzy sets of sectors. Now, instead of a continuous range, the system works with a set of discrete values of orientation angles that is much easier to use for fast decision making and logical operations.

Unlike a camera's memory, the brain remembers the world as it is, not as it appears. When human think about the world, they recall sequences of patterns that correspond to the way the objects in the world are and how they behave, not how they appear through any particular sense at any point in time. The sequences by which they experience objects in the world reflect the invariant structure of the world itself. The world's structure determines the order in which the human experience parts of the world.

The computer vision system, equipped with a set of Color and Size Measuring symbolic devices, can use qualitative values, obtained from such

Figure 13. Quantification of an Image and Active Fusion: 2½-D Sketch as a Primary Network Structure. Primary continuous information -- image intensity converts into two 1/2-D Sketch, which is a quantified picture. The sketch looks like a graph on a more abstract level. Connection to other symbolic devices (Size Measuring and Color) creates active fusion. Such a graph structure implicitly carries information about the part of the image: orientation, color, sizes. The mechanisms of cortical columns work similarly.

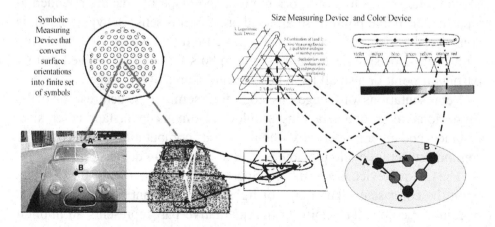

devices, for logical operations. This way such system actually "understands" color and proportions.

Orientation also can be represented in a symbolic form, if there is a symbolic space, which quantifies a continuous set of directional angles into a finite set of sections. (The same way color symbolic space quantifies the continuous scale of light waves by a few colors.) Orientation can be represented this way in a symbolic form and used for further logical operations. J.J. Koenderink and Van Doorn in their work (June 1995), related to the Pictorial Relief, described such a feature space, which is a Symbolic space. Arrows on the drawings of Marr's 2½-D sketch are also symbols of the orientation of surfaces.

From this position, structures similar to Marr's 2½-D sketch appear in the cortical area V1. Hubel described the granular organization of the columns in that cortical area. It gives color + depth + orientation at one point within the hypercolumn. The 2½-d sketch is simply a real-world image converted to a primary network structure on a quasi-regular grid in V1, where nodes are cortical columns in V1. Every such node has a set of associated "symbolic" meanings (color + depth + orientation).

The goal of the lower part of the vision system, which starts from the retina and ends with the V1 primary visual area, is to bring a complete set of image features into the cortex. The influence of higher levels means some selectivity, and it can make the loss of information. It either should be minimal, or it should not be at all.

Most probably, the wrong ideas about domination of bottom-up unsupervised processes in vision originated from the early vision research that focused mainly on retinal processes and processes in the optic tract and cortical area V1. This area is displays primary visual information, converted to a granular "symbolic" form, to the higher areas of the brain. The higher areas do further analysis of the image. Therefore, a natural image processing requires a conversion to a structure, rather than precise computations of a 3-D model.

Here we came to a critical point about invariant recognition. If we look at Figure 14, we can see three entirely different figures. However, all three can be easily placed in the same class, because all three can produce the same abstract derivative graphs. The ability to derive the same graphs automatically classifies images as exemplars of the same class.

Representation of object by abstract derivative structures is truly invariant to shift, rotation, and scale. The same object taken in different views can be recognized as the same (See Figure 14, right) if various views still produce

Figure 14. Three funny figures on the left appear to be different. But all three can be easily classified as related to the same class because each produces the same derivative graph. The three abstract figures on the right show the same idea, but with different positions of the same object. There is nothing new in this idea. Structural methods are as old as the statistical ones.

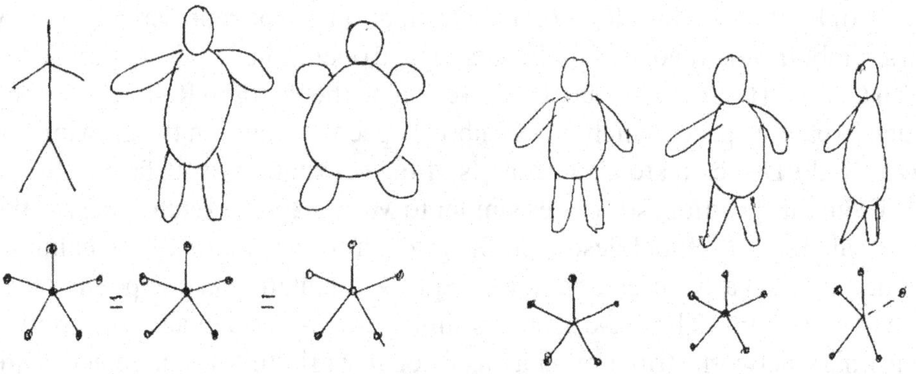

the same graph. In case when different perspectives do not match exactly, the graphs could be matched in the most part.

If significant parts of graphs are the same, we still can recognize the object. And if different views of the same object produce different graphs, we can link such graphs to the symbol, which denotes such object. The object will now be invariably recognized from different views. There is absolutely no need for the precise recreation of the entire 3-D object from its various 2-D views.

Primary structures usually are not compatible. This is a perfect reason to switch from structural to statistical approach. However, it also does not guarantee the correct results. Invariant recognition requires a separation of figure from ground, derivation of number of structures and complex decision processes. This cannot be done with a single method for real-world images. In general, it requires a complex systematic environment.

It also answers the question why a real-world image cannot be described in words. In many cases simply no word exists in a human language for the description of a particular component of the image. Such cases are handled with implicit labeling, using a mechanism of the model and symbolic spaces that pack similar structures into symbols. Human vision works the same way. Our visual "vocabulary" is much richer than our written and spoken the language. However, as soon as a combination of sounds or letters is associated with such a symbol, it becomes a new word and a new concept of the human language.

In general, a semantic description can be done only on the highest level of Informational Pathway. There is no way to transform a primary network structure directly into the semantic description, skipping the intermediary levels of the Informational Pathway.

The solution of Image Understanding problem is the creation of dynamic multilevel hierarchical knowledge models, which can generate and support decisions, and efficiently resolve ambiguity and uncertainty in the real-world images. Such models can work only when there is a way to label such models without explicit labeling.

The concept of Symbolic Space is introduced to solve this problem. Symbolic Space is a dual structure that combines some closed distributed space split by the set of fuzzy regions, and discrete set of symbols equivalent to the cores of regions represented as points in the Certainty dimension.

For classification of a real-world object, a more flexible representation is needed that breaks rigidity assumption. Such a representation must allow for the structure of an object so that a tree or a graph can serve as a "class signature" of a particular form or shape. It requires switching from the shape descriptors based on the computations of absolute values to a relational, structural description of an object regarding network-symbolic theory. Segmentation and hierarchical clustering of an object or a shape with the set of multilevel receptive fields is an initial step in this direction that allows for the conversion of continuous and absolute image information into a relational network-symbolic model. (See Figures 15-18)

Having in mind that this mathematical apparatus combines both quantitative and qualitative parts with the ability to transfer between them, there are no restrictions on the methods that can be used in the quantitative part, except that the outcomes must be converted into an implicit symbolic form with the mechanism of fuzzy sets.

The foveal system can be considered an acuity window that moves within the visual buffer to build a spatial map, which also is a scene graph. The foveal system treats the object in its center as a figure, while the peripheral vision gives a broader picture of the entire scene, and helps with motion control. An object tracking system keeps the analyzed object in the center of the fovea. A tracking mechanism reduces object motion to scaling and rotation. The former can be used for disambiguating spatial order of visual scene, while the latter reveals the 3-dimensional structure of an object. In high-quality color movies, rotating objects sometimes display stunning 3-dimensional effects without

Figure 15. Cortical column as a semiotic device

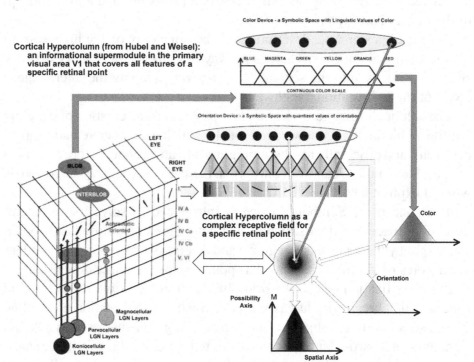

Figure 16. The concept of a receptive field can be spatially represented as a fuzzy set. A "complex" receptive field spatially clusters receptive fields from a lower level, thus providing a hierarchy of information processing in a larger spatial area of an image. This repeated multilevel hierarchical structure allows for multi-level hierarchical spatial clustering and space partitioning upon certain criteria, such as, for instance, derived values of the features as symbols on a particular level. The clustering has a spatial nature, and there are no restrictions on types or numbers of processing features that are outputs of receptive fields.

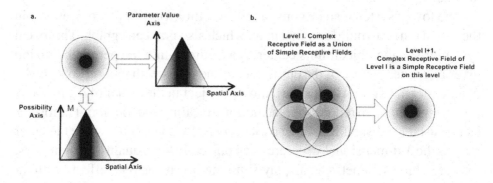

Figure 17. a. Logarithmic Scale Device in a 2-dimensional case; b. Hierarchically clustered receptive fields achieve the same results, forming a Fuzzy Pyramid. Such a structure can be used for qualitative logical evaluation of sizes without precise calculations.

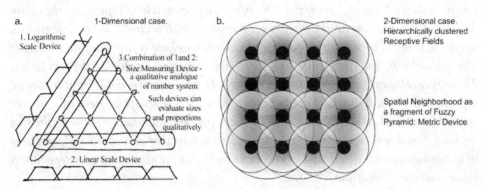

any stereo equipment. The same or similar neural mechanism, which derives 3-dimensional information from relative disparity, also derives 3-dimensional information from motion. The relational change of appearance of an object is the primary source of 3-dimensional information about this object.

The equivalent of interaction between peripheral and foveal systems in the network-symbolic system is achieved via interaction between Visual and Object Buffers and top-level system of Visual Intelligence. This is shown in Figure 19.

Figure 19 shows the process of separation of distinctive regions in the visual buffer. Bottom-up fine-scale separation of areas can rarely be sufficient for real world images if applied to the whole image without having clear criteria of how further to combine obtained neighboring regions into objects. Just on an individual scale, an object or a pattern can be perceived as an object or a pattern rather than a set of neighboring regions.

Therefore, a region of interest, where the object or pattern can be located, must be established first. A large receptive field can roughly identify presence or absence of particular object features via statistics of the covered region. Repeating this operation on the lower levels for the hierarchically connected receptive fields with the selected features will narrow down the area of interest to the one that contains selected features/symbols.

Perceptual grouping is one of the most important processes in human vision, and it binds visual information into meaningful patterns and structures. In

Figure 18. A simplified abstract idea of Logical Filtering as a combination of qualitative and quantitative methods. If a relational difference between the numeric values X and Y of an individual feature of receptive fields A and B are "small," fields A and B can be considered similar. This allows for concatenating or clustering receptive fields A and B. A receptive field of a higher spatial level represents the union A U B, as it covers an area with similar features. Such a clustering or integration upon the criteria of similarity can hierarchically include a region of an image. If a relational difference is significant, there is no way to concatenate the two fields. There is a relation between the values or symbols of the two fields, and it can be represented by an individual symbol other than "=." A receptive field of a higher spatial level marked with such a symbol can represent a boundary between the two regions. Since a receptive field is a spatial structure that can carry different sets of symbols/features, it is possible to choose the basis for clustering and separation upon a single or multiple features.

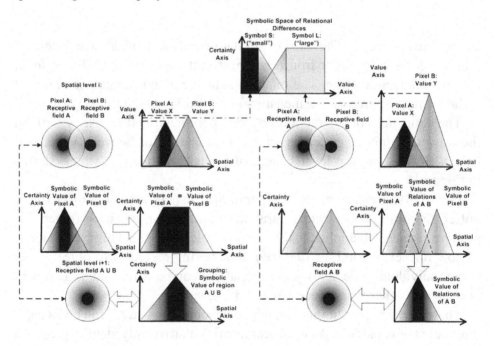

the network-symbolic, it happens with the help of Linker that links receptive fields with similar features/symbols into coherent structures.

Fuzzy top-down processes can best fit the informational processes in the visual buffer and led to the localization of patterns and placing relevant objects/patterns into object buffer, where they can be analyzed on a fine scale as separate entities.

Figure 19. The process of separation of distinctive regions in the visual buffer. For rigid bodies, (a) neighbor lower-level receptive fields must be connected to compose a coherent spatial structure. The obtained structure can be placed into the object buffer and analyzed as a separate entity.

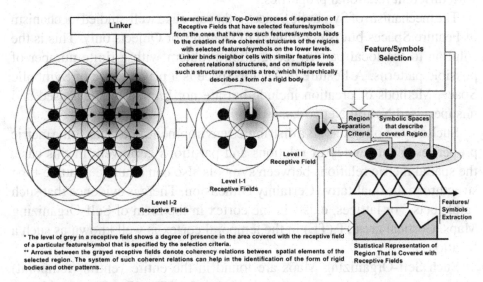

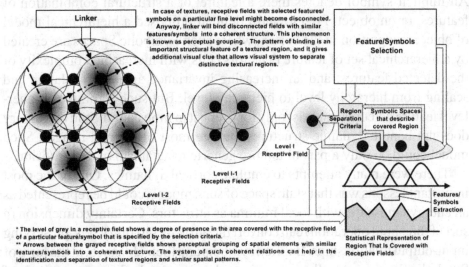

(top=a; bottom=b)

In the case of textures (b), the receptive fields with selected features may be spatially remote. As a part of the perceptual grouping process, Linker will bind the remote receptive fields that have similar features into a coherent structure. The pattern of binding is an essential structural element of textured regions and can help to identify similar texture and separate textured areas with different relational properties.

The mechanism of Symbolic Spaces is the same as a well-studied mechanism of Feature Spaces but is not limited to Features or Objects only. This is the solution to the local pattern recognition problem with a finite number of possible patterns. A Feature or Vector Space is a private case of Symbolic Space. Methods of creation include but are not limited to supervised and unsupervised Neural Networks.

Such a Symbolic Space is a distributed environment, and it has some metric properties. Equivalency of relations and partitions is proven. In this case, the spatial metric relations between symbols also can emulate a lattice-type structure in the qualitative Certainty Dimension. There is evidence that such "alphabets," or lattices, exists in the cortex in the form of Self-Organizing Maps. Cortical area IT (TE) in the temporal cortex is well known as such a location.

Such Self-Organizing Maps are found in the entire ventral (temporal) pathway from the primary visual area V1 to IT (TE) (See Figures 20-21). An implicit symbol denotes there a feature, or a structural combination of features, or an object. Poggio and Edelman proposed a hierarchical model of object recognition in the cortex, where such Symbolic Spaces are created by a hierarchical set of feature detectors cells with increasing complexity of the detected features, and an increasing invariance against translation and scaling from hierarchy level to hierarchy level. But such a complex higher-level feature detector can exist only for a repeat in time pattern, and this theory does not handle dynamic structures that are most of the real images. Such model could be only a part of a more generic mechanism of active vision.

There were many attempts to emulate cortical dynamics. One of the most important lessons was that state space of such models could be represented as an energy landscape with local minima as attractors. Certainty dimension (a sort of threshold operation) can convert the attractors to fuzzy sets, preserving input-output relationships. Implicit symbols and their alphabets in the form of Symbolic Spaces naturally emerge in such networks. In this way, methods of Computational intelligence can transform energy landscape into the relational symbolic representation.

Figure 20. Implicit symbols and their alphabets on the lower levels of perception

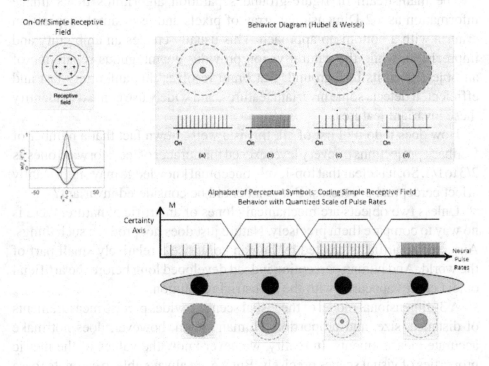

Figure 21. Another look at the cortical area IT (TE): implicit perceptual alphabets

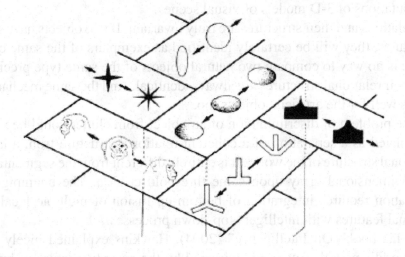

The mainstream of figure-ground separation algorithms treats image information as a 2-Dimensional array of pixels and uses simple separation criteria with a bottom-up approach. This usually creates an ambiguity and imprecision, while the natural vision provides unambiguous separation of an object from its background. But brain resolves this ambiguity fast and efficient. It detects some invariant features, and widely use context to identify these invariant features.

How does it do it? First of all, this is a well-known fact that a number of feedback projections on every level exceed the number of feed-forward ones as 2/3 to 1/3. So, it is clear that top-level conceptual knowledge may significantly affect perceptual processes. But what could be considered invariant?

Unless two objects are mechanical clones of an artificial nature, there is no way to compare them precisely. Nature just does not produce such things. Any precise artifacts created by human comprise a relatively small part of the world. And human perception indeed developed long before the artificial object clones appeared with the industrial revolution.

A 3-dimensional model of the visual scene provides precise measurements of distance, size, and proportion. Human vision, however, does not make accurate measurements. In reality, we never know the values of the metric properties of visual scenes precisely. But we are always able to estimate these properties in relative terms.

The brain uses principles of relative representation and processing of perceptual and conceptual information. Natural image processing requires a conversion of images into cognitive, relational structures instead of precise computations of 3-D models of visual scenes.

Relations and their structures are truly invariant. If two objects have same structures, they will be certainly identified as exemplars of the same class. There is no way to compare two natural objects of the same type precisely. But their relational structures are always identical. And the same mechanism works well for the artificial objects too.

The problem of discrimination of an object from clutter could be rather formulated as a separation of a coherent relational structure from a larger relational structure of the world. It is entirely different from the segmentation of 2-Dimensional array upon some threshold criteria. The unambiguous separation requires integration of bottom-up fusion of multiple local and regional features with intelligent top-down processes.

In his book" On Intelligence" (2004), Hawkins explained nicely how real world's nested structure is mirrored by the nested structure of human cortex: " The cortex has a learning algorithm that naturally finds whatever hierarchical structure exists and captures it. When structure cannot be found, we are thrown into confusion.

Information arrives into the brain as a sequence of patterns. A sequence is a set of patterns that accompany each other, although not always in a fixed order. The cortex wants to learn those sequences that occur over and over again. Learning sequences is the most necessary ingredient for forming invariant representations of real-world objects.

The fact that certain input patterns repeat time and again is what lets a cortical region know that those experiences are caused by a real object in the world. Predictability is the very definition of reality. A predictable sequence of patterns must be part of a larger object that exists. When we assign a name to something, we do so because a set of features consistently travels together. Real-world objects can be concrete or abstract. The brain treats abstract and real objects in the same way.

Therefore, the brain can store sequences of sequences. Each region of the cortex learns sequences, develops what Hawkins calls "names" for the sequences it knows and passes these names to the next areas higher in the cortical hierarchy. Each cortical area has a name for each sequence it knows. This "name" is a group of cells whose collective firing represents the set of objects in the sequence.

These cells remain active as long as the sequence is playing, and it is this "name" that is passed up to the next region in the hierarchy. In this fashion, a predictable sequence of events gets identified with a "name"— a consistent pattern of cell firing. This happens over and over again as we go up the hierarchical pyramid.

By collapsing predictable sequences into "named objects" at each region in our hierarchy, we achieve more and more stability the higher we go. This creates invariant representations." (Hawkins, 2004, p.130)

Information passes through the cortical areas via many levels of complexity: from primitive visual features to more complex structures, then to objects and their classes, then to action, events, and spatial situations, and to elaborate coherent scenarios. It is like an information path where information converts from primitive features into complex cognitive structures.

This repeats on multiple levels of information processing. It is well known that brain connections are going from primary visual area V1 to prefrontal cortical areas that that are responsible for intelligence and decision-making.

This idea is shown on the Figure 22. This path is not straightforward, and it goes via the multilevel sets of feed forward links finishing in the intermediary areas. It is a known fact that certain areas are responding to certain information,

Figure 22. Information path in the brain from primitive features to complex cognitive structures. Feedback projections on every level create a context system that resolves the ambiguity.

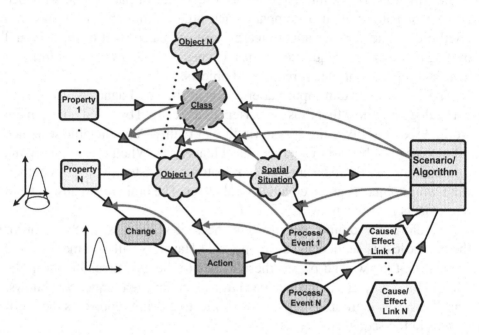

like for instance to human faces, etc. Each area is specialized in the processing of certain information, and this goes from level to level.

For instance, low-level visual areas can recognize primitive features, while the areas above recognize objects, etc. This is evident that brain hierarchically structures information on multiple levels from primitive features to complex scenes, somehow memorizing only essential repeated invariant patterns.

If hierarchical processing of information in the brain is a well-recognized fact, much less attention is usually paid to the fact that feedback projections take at least 2/3 of all projections on every level, and only 1/3 of all projections are feed forward. This means that context drives the recognition process from the levels above. And this is also an Achilles heel of most existing methods, one of the major factors of their failures, because the context is not considered.

The volume of stored knowledge can be pretty large. But human can only experience a subset of the world at any moment in time. And a person can process only a limited amount of relevant information in a sequential order. This is a limitation of the human processing system, and it is well known that a regular person can actually control just a few points/concepts in their mind at the same time. For more, a crew is needed. What if a computer system could control more points than an average human does?

From the first sight, looks like human brain fights with computational complexity. This is true, but only partially. The processing capability may be limited with resources that are needed to concentrate on the problem. The recourses that activate relevant information are limited, and focus of attention is lost. If someone is tired and cannot concentrate, the problem cannot be solved.

The overall picture leads us to a simple conclusion: practical recognition won't work if a context system is not involved. And real world situations may require high-level modelas that go up high to cognitive knowledge processes. If the context is lacking – the results are ambiguous, and recognition fails. Therefore, we may need to build an efficient cognitive knowledge system that drives contextual processes for perception to work.

Also, humans are helpless in their intelligent tasks not only without language but also without external carriers like as paper in the past and the computers now. This is a limitation of human memory mechanisms that requires external carriers for expressing models as visuals or language constructs.

We will show how such Semiotics systems possess capabilities to represent knowledge in a unified format. And if making them active, implementing certain methods and architecture, they can not only learn but also derive knowledge, automatically order it, and build new relevant prediction models.

REFERENCES

Burnod, Y. (1991). An Adaptive Neural Network: *Cerebral Cortex*. Academic Press.

Grossberg, S., & Levine, D. S. (1987). Neural dynamics of attentionally modulated Pavlovian conditioning: Blocking, inter-stimulus interval, and secondary reinforcement. *Psychobiology (Austin, Tex.)*, *15*(3), 195–240.

Hawkins, J., & Blakeslee, S. (2004) *On Intelligence*. St. Martin's Griffin.

Hebb, D. O. (1949). *The Organization of Behavior*. New York: Wiley & Sons.

Hubel, D. H., & Wiesel, T. N. (2004). *Brain and Visual Perception: The Story of a 25-Year Collaboration*. Oxford University Press. doi:10.1093/acprof:oso/9780195176186.001.0001

Hubel, D. H., & Wiesel, T. N. (2004). *Brain and Visual Perception: The Story of a 25-Year Collaboration*. Oxford University Press. doi:10.1093/acprof:oso/9780195176186.001.0001

Koenderink, J. J., & van Doorn, A. J. (1995, June). Relief: Pictorial and Otherwise. *Image and Vision Computing*, *13*(5), 321–334. doi:10.1016/0262-8856(95)99719-H

Kosslyn, S. (1996). *Image and Brain*. MIT Press.

Mountcastle, V. (1978). An Organizing Principle for Cerebral Function: The Unit Model and the Distributed System. In G. M. Edelman & V. B. Mountcastle (Eds.), *The Mindful Brain*. Cambridge, MA: MIT Press.

Perlovsky, L. I. (2004). Integrating Language, and Cognition. *IEEE Connections*, *2*(2), 8-12.

Perlovsky, L. I. (2010). Neural Mechanisms of the Mind, Aristotle, Zadeh, & fMRI. *IEEE Transactions on Neural Networks*, *21*(5), 718–733. doi:10.1109/TNN.2010.2041250 PMID:20199934

Tanaka, K. (1996). *Inferotemporal cortex and object vision*. Academic Press.

Zadeh, L. A. (1975). The Concept of a Linguistic Variable and its Application to Approximate Reasoning. *Information Sciences*, *8*(3), 199–249. doi:10.1016/0020-0255(75)90036-5

Chapter 2
Topological Semiotic Knowledge Representation

ABSTRACT

This chapter describes cognitive models that organize implicit symbols into meaningful relational network structures. With an understanding of implicit symbols, there is evidence that informational processes on the cortical level can create and maintain multileveled hierarchically nested graphs and diagram – like structures. This topological model reflects hierarchically ordered knowledge of world structure and processes. Suggested models reflect systems, and they have structural relations embedded in the model. Ability to generate on fly new meaningful graphs and diagrams allows for modeling phenomena of intelligence like analogies, conceptual blending, and many others.

INTRODUCTION

Hebbian learning is studied pretty well, possibly due to its mechanism based on the adaptive statistics. Much less attention was paid in the past to other mechanisms such as for instance Pavlovian reflex (1927), which links neural assemblies that were activated simultaneously or sequentially.

In April 1903, Pavlov presented his early work on the conditioned reflex to the International Congress of Medicine, Madrid. In his book "Natural Science and the Brain," he proposed that the conditioned reflex developed through the action of two types of brain process. The first of these was a "temporary

DOI: 10.4018/978-1-5225-2431-1.ch002

union, i.e., the establishment of a new connection in the conducting paths". In 1909, Pavlov proposed a theory of associative learning.

Briefly, the brain can establish associations between separate areas that were activated either simultaneously, or within a short period. If this is a stable pattern, it will be repeated. And this is a great chance that such a repeated pattern will be observed in future with a high degree of certainty.

Conditional reflex demonstrates the human capability to capture the connection between cause and effect. Pavlov showed that even very artificial sequence of events might create such a link.

There is some misconception on how this mechanism works and how this connection can be established, at least on the modeling level. Some models assume that this remote link may be set after activation repeats. But such a model can work only for local links. For remote links, a fast connection between the remote areas must be established from the very beginning. Then it can be either kept or disappear if this activation was random and not repeated regularly.

Such links form relational structures, and from the informational standpoint, such a structure looks like a graph or a diagram.

I. Pavlov (1927) discovered reflex as a learning mechanism, and D. Hebb (1949) discovered how such learning happens. The mainstream of research was focused mainly on the models of Hebbian learning. But learning is just one of the many processes in the brain, and such learning models just don't seem to capture the essence of biological systems. There is always something organic missing, like, for instance, attention – a top-down control process. The list can be continued.

Vector space or symbolic space is not enough for the explanation of informational processes related to the image understanding. Understanding cannot be reduced to recognition, the same way as intelligence cannot be reduced to memory recall. It requires such a computational mechanism that not only learns but also works with the dynamic spatial relationships and structures, actually allowing fast creation of new dynamic structures.

An implicit symbol is an equivalent to a recognized feature, or a structural combination of features, or an object. In a more general sense, such symbol denotes a pattern. The pattern is a structure, repeated in time, or space. Therefore, in the Network-Symbolic systems, a feature or an object can be identical to the node of such system, where such node can also represent a symbol, or a predicate, or a pattern, or a lower-level structure.

New results of brain research suggest that the informational processes exist rather on the cortical level, between the groups of neurons. For instance, a process links together separated cortical areas that were activated simultaneously, or within a short period. If such activation repeated, the relationship becomes permanent.

One possible candidate for linking/binding cortical information into a coherent structure is a temporal synchronization. Also, brain researchers showed that synchronized neural assembly in the hippocampus support permanent cortical memory formation, allowing cortical neural assemblies to interact, and modifying their synaptic connectivity. Therefore, the hippocampus can copy and create stable structures in memory, working as a linker for the entire brain.

Independently of the underlying physical processes, linking is a graph/diagrammatic operation on the informational level, and links create a graph/diagram-type structure. As we can see from Figures 1-2, the synchronous pattern of information in the brain can be represented as graph/diagrammatic-type structures on the informational level. Such structures are dynamic by their nature. But repeated structures become patterns, and such patterns can be saved in memory.

The entire system of such cortical graphs/networks is a Network-Symbolic system, and it may act as a Distributed or Spatial Turing Machine. Such machine differs from a regular Symbolic Turing Machine. Networks take the place of symbols, and they are memory and control part.

This means that at the abstract informational level brain works with relational structures such as graphs/diagrams. Such representation provides models and intelligent, systematic operations, which can work with dynamic spatial patterns. Implicit symbols and their alphabets can be represented as

Figure 1. Energy landscape of a neural network with local minima (left) as attractors (center). The introduction of the certainty dimension converts resonance attractors into granular fuzzy sets, preserving the same topological relationships (right). Dual nature of normalized fuzzy sets automatically converts such a map into a symbolic space.

Symbolic Spaces. The next layer is relational: graphs, trees, logic, grammars are based on nodes, implicitly labeled with such symbols.

Such theoretical mechanism is called Model Space. It carries links and relations between symbols - cores of fuzzy units in the symbolic spaces; represents some diagram/graph model; provides logical mechanisms; can change itself, performing graph operations; other symbolic and model spaces can be further derived from such model space.

The combination of Symbolic and Model Spaces is a Network-Symbolic system:

1. It can create models without explicit labels and external symbols. Labels and symbols just exist there implicitly in the form of Symbolic Spaces and can be created and modified on the fly.
2. Induction, deduction, other methods of algorithmic learning and higher-level reasoning are simply means of graph transformations within a single framework.
3. Logic is simply a way of linking and ordering such networks under the laws of search-synthesis-analysis.
4. Continuous methods of machine learning, classification and analogy provide necessary transformations of continuous information into the graph-like discrete structures, used by the methods from the previous paragraph.
5. The mechanism handles redundancies, packing similarities into structures, and replacing redundant parts with their symbols. Space can have its symbol. Repeated structures can have their symbol in a symbolic space.
6. Spaces provide inherent modularity and hierarchy. This reduces the computational volume to normal.
7. Linker process and attention mechanism are "biologically" necessary for such system of working spaces.
8. Such a network-symbolic system is a "self-operating." The combination of bottom-up and top-down method leads to the situation where graph/diagrammatic structures can create another, conceptual derivative graphs/diagrams.

Such Network-Symbolic system is a Spatial/Distributed Turing Machine that differs from a regular Symbolic Turing Machine. Networks take the place of symbols on tape and control part. They are both data and algorithms simultaneously, and they can rewrite themselves being a memory and the control part simultaneously. (See Figure 2)

Vision system evolved in vertebrates not only as a simple recognition system, but also as a sensory system for reaching, grasping, and other activities tightly integrated with the motion system. In advanced creatures, it became a component of prediction function, allowing the creation of sophisticated environmental models and action planning. Fast information processing and decision making is vital and requires reduction of informational complexity. For that, relational Network-symbolic brain system uses symbols, hierarchical compression, and selective attention.

NETWORK-SYMBOLIC SYSTEM IN THE BRAIN

Accumulated information gives the opportunity to formulate two important hypotheses:

Hypothesis I: A Network-Symbolic System in the Brain

1. An emulated network-symbolic system exists in the brain. Networks of neurons provide an environment that works as "hardware" for this "software" system.

Figure 2. Representation of physical (left) and informational (right) processes between synchronously activated neural assemblies. Complex neural dynamics represent a graph-type structure on the cortical level (a similar case: complex dynamics in the semiconductor junctions of a microprocessor merely represent Boolean 1-s or 0-s).

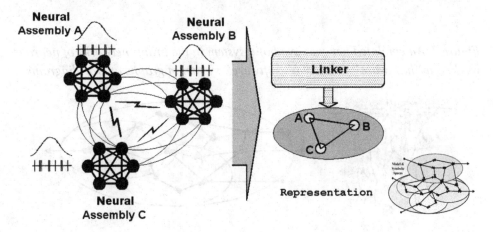

2. Such a network environment is "systematic." Graphs and diagrams can represent the models and processes in that environment.
3. Models in such networks can drive processes, create other models. This is what we may call intelligence.
4. Such graphs and networks are sorts of cortical programs, or "cortical software," and Network-Symbolic system is a kind of an operational system in the cortex (See Figure 3). The components are everywhere, the location of top-level abstract derivative structures that can make abstract intelligent operations is the prefrontal and frontal cortex.

Hypothesis II: Derivative Structures and Their Role in Recognition

1. Derivative Structures are abstract model structures that are created, or derived from, other model structures.
2. Invariant classification of images is achieved via matching their derivative structures rather than their primary structures.
3. Abstract derivative structures play a crucial role in intelligence. The capacity of frontal areas in human brain provides the power for creating such abstract structures that separate humans from animals.

Graphs and diagrams reflect the natural way that a person produces models in the brain.

Graphs and diagrams can represent general knowledge and informational models because:

Figure 3. An emulated network-symbolic system in the brain: networks of neurons work as a "hardware" for such a "software" system of graphs and/or diagrams

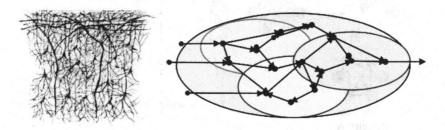

1. A point is a qualitative abstract model, expressing decision and certainty about something.
2. A system is the most generic concept of knowledge representation.
3. A graph (network) is an ordered set of related points and can represent a qualitative abstract model -- system.

The relational graph can be represented as a set of nodes, their connections, and relations between them. Relation itself becomes a node. Qualitative relation requires for identification a discrete structure like, for instance, lattice, that carries order - a basic pattern of relationship. Logical level is the level, which qualitatively describes such structures. Therefore, for the structural representation, logic is simply the way of linking or ordering such structure. The quantitative relation can be identified on some scale.

The graph has its dual - a diagram. A diagram is a tessellation of a planar area such that it is completely covered by atomic two-dimensional regions or elements. If we replace points of the graph with some distributed representation, preserving the same relations, we convert it to a diagram.

The infamous Pattern Recognition problem can never be solved for real-world images in a general statement but can be successfully solved as subtasks of the Image Understanding problem because:

1. A pattern is a discernible coherent system based on the intended interrelationship of parts and can be observed as a frequent or widespread incidence.
2. A graph model of the system, used as the pattern, therefore, should be stable.
3. Any real-world image rarely meets these requirements. Just as the system presented in the picture is dynamic and changeable, so is its structural model. Only some components having stable structures from image to image can be recognized as patterns.
4. The ambiguity and uncertainty in the real-world images are resolved in many cases with the help of top-down processes that involve higher-level knowledge.

Cognitive science teaches that knowledge has a highly organized structure and is represented at a higher level in a symbolic form. At a shallow level, knowledge has sub-symbolic, distributed representation as a network of nodes. When software developers create a program system, the first thing is to identify data types for that system. Assume that the system must work with the real-world knowledge in a generic form. Would it be possible to describe all the real world objects and processes as a finite set of formalized information categories, it might help.

The solution of Image Understanding problem is the creation of active multilevel hierarchical networks, which can generate and support some decisions, making such networks equivalent to a simulation model, and actually resolving ambiguity and uncertainty in the real-world images.

GENERIC KNOWLEDGE REPRESENTATION MECHANISM

To make knowledge models working automatically, we have first to find a way to label such models without explicit labeling. The concept of Symbolic Space was introduced for the solution of this problem. Mathematically, it can be formulated as a dual structure, combining:

1. Some closed distributed space, split into a set of fuzzy regions with certain topological properties between the cores of the regions;
2. A discrete set of symbols represented as points in the certainty dimension that are equivalent to the cores of the fuzzy areas.

The mechanism of Symbolic Spaces is the same as a well-studied mechanism of Feature Spaces but is not limited to Features or Objects only. This is the solution to the local pattern recognition problem with a finite number of possible patterns. A Feature / Vector Space is a particular case of Symbolic Space. Methods of creation Symbolic Spaces include, but are not limited with:

- Fuzzy ART and ARTMAP;
- SOM, SVM, LVQ, Boltzmann Machines, etc.;
- Adaptive splines;
- Quantum/Holographic NN methods;
- Radial Basis Function Neural Networks;
- Other supervised and unsupervised NN methods, able to create energy landscapes with resonance attractors.

The introduction of Certainty Dimension converts resonance attractors in neural networks into the granular fuzzy sets, preserving the same topological relationships. Here we have a Symbolic Space, where symbols denote multi-dimensional combinations of the features. Regarding MPEG-7 it is equivalent to the set of descriptors. (MPEG-7, 2017).

Learning in distributed, continuous environment is the process of dynamic creation of transfer function, that maps input to the desired output, and that means that we can create new and modify old symbols on the fly.

However, by itself, vector space, or symbolic space is not enough for the image understanding.

In the general case, understanding cannot be reduced to recognition, the same way as intelligence cannot be reduced to memory recall. To handle the reality, we must handle with dynamic structural models. We need another mechanism that not only learns but also works with relationships and structures, allowing the creation of new structures from the old ones.

Such mechanism called Model Space was introduced in author's works (Kuvich, 2003-2006). The Model Space:

- Carries links and relations between symbols - cores of fuzzy units in symbolic spaces;
- Represents some diagram/ graph model dually;
- Provides logical mechanisms and can change itself, performing graph/ diagrammatic operations;
- Other symbolic and model spaces can be further derived from such model space.

Regarding MPEG-7, it is an equivalent to the description schema. A combination of symbolic and model spaces can create labeled models without explicit symbols.

Spaces can be connected to or can include other spaces. All possible diagrammatic, graph and topological operations and transformations are available. This mechanism handles redundancies, packing similarities into structures. This works like a giant data compression machine. Similar parts of different graphs create symbolic spaces and replace redundant parts with their symbols.

Other computational models and mechanisms can be easily emulated in such dual environment:

- Conceptual mathematics;
- Minsky's frames;

- Gardendorf's conceptual spaces;
- Edelman's reentrant maps;
- Bayesian networks;
- Graph rewriting systems;
- Sowa's conceptual graphs;
- Pierce-Vienna Diagrams;
- UML diagrams;
- Schema Learning Systems;
- Marr's 2½D sketch;
- Informational Pathway.

The advantages of the proposed mechanism are:

- It can create models without explicit labels and external symbols. Labels and symbols just exist there implicitly in the form of the Symbolic Spaces and can be created and modified on the fly.
- Induction, deduction, other methods of algorithmic learning and higher level reasoning are now simply methods of graph transformations within a single framework. It gives the opportunity to apply symbolic algorithms in the network environment, rewriting them into their network representation that makes them simpler and more natural.
- Continuous methods of machine learning, classification and analogy provide necessary transformations of continuous information into the graph-like discrete structures that can naturally coexist with the intelligent methods of graph transformation from the paragraph above.
- Spaces provide needed modularity that allows reducing the computational volume to the level that makes such mechanism practically realizable.

The system of spaces creates more abstract derivative structures, such as syntactic ones, that act as "measurement devices," or algorithms. Distributed methods give ways of handling with uncertainty, representing it spatially. Dual representation naturally combines methods of classification, analogy, and machine learning, together with induction, deduction and other methods of higher level reasoning within a single framework. (See Figures 4-5). Here they are algorithms of transformations of the networks under the laws of search-synthesis-analysis. Logic is simply a way of linking and ordering such networks.

SYSTEM THINKING AND SYSTEMATIC KNOWLEDGE REPRESENTATION

During more than 50 past years brain and nervous system were intensively studied, and Cognitive Science and Brain Sciences have accumulated a significant volume of information about the brain and nervous system. But there is still a large gap between pretty well studied physical processes in neurons and top level informational processes.

Methods of higher-level knowledge representation are based mainly on the theories of symbolic math and natural language. Such representations have no connection to the neuroscience and brain research. Without a proper theory of knowledge, there was a strong tendency to substitute models of

Figure 4. Graph transformations are a necessary component of algorithms. This picture shows a simple example of graph transformations via a morphological operation using a sort of graph grammar. Even more sophisticated "intelligent" operations, like induction, deduction, etc., follow the rules of graph transformations, and the same idea, presented in this picture, works in all instances.

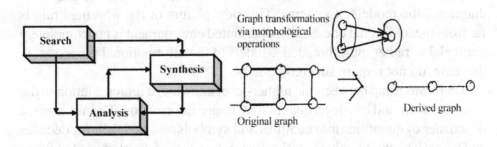

Figure 5. Language and related phenomena appear as a serialization in such networks. When smaller disconnected abstract model structures, independently placed somewhere in memory, come together in a certain place in a particular order, they can create a larger, complete network model.

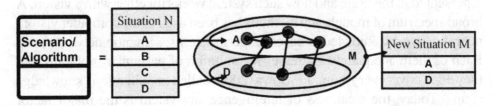

informational processes with the models of physical processes in the neural "hardware."

But such models just don't seem to capture the essence of informational processes in the biological systems. Physical processes are not identical to informational processes. An intricate pattern of energy activity in the semiconductors of a microchip is described as a complex set of partial differential equations. But on the informational level, it represents Boolean 0-s and 1-s.

If differential equations were used instead of Boolean logic, digital computers would remain a theory. Similarly, for our goals, instead of emulating physical processes in the cortex, it would be better to find out informational representation of intelligent operations in the cortex.

The situation started changing only in the recent years with the significant development of multi-agent systems, methods of computational intelligence, and theories of visual languages, graph- and diagram-based representations and other natural representations of knowledge. New trends in the brain and cognitive research shift the emphasis from the processes in neural networks to the processes in the cortical areas.

The research shows the ability of the human brain to emulate dynamic multilevel hierarchical relational networks that are equivalent to graph- or diagrammatic models of systems. This new picture of the working brain is far from the traditional one. Such a distributed environment is not completely parallel, but rather multithreaded. Models of the informational processes, in this case, do not require supercomputers.

There was a gap between the higher-level knowledge representation in the symbolic form and low-level quantitative image information. The mechanism of transfer of quantities into qualities and symbols was not clear for decades and became apparent only recently after many years of development of fuzzy set theory by L. Zadeh and others.

There are well-known facts today that visual areas project to the prefrontal and frontal cortex, which is the carrier of knowledge and intelligence. Feedback projections drive attention and separation of figure from ground. But there is still no widely accepted theory of how knowledge and intelligence can be represented in the brain and how such system works together with a vision. A broad spectrum of models and methods has been used in the computer vision: neural networks, knowledge bases, expert systems, semantic networks, etc. Each of them adequately addresses the solution of particular problems, but they don't cover everything. J.F. Sowa (2000) called this situation "knowledge soup." Today, the weakness of intelligence subsystem is the major factor responsible for failures of the computer vision systems and image/video understanding applications.

Lack of a unifying representation of knowledge has led to hybrid vision systems combining heuristics and different approaches. There are a few custom Image Understanding systems, and CAD-based, Model-based, Context-based, Object-based vision systems. They are based mostly on the similar to D. Marr's ideas (1982) about 3-D image as a recognition model. Human vision does not work this way. Rather it gives us a sort of understanding of visual scene with an understanding of ranges and distances.

Enough data were accumulated from the brain lesions, fMRI, PET. Existing theories of perception can give a very general picture of possible information processing on the level of the entire brain, mapped to the particular cortical areas. But they lacked the representation of data and informational processes on the intermediary levels between the whole brain and neural cell assemblies.

Cognitive and computer sciences have accumulated multiple models of intelligent processes. It would not be completely accurate to say that brain use such models. But the right statement is that those models reflect processes in the brain.

Assume that we need to design an intelligent system, where the human mind is a prototype. To start building any information system, we need to provide its specifications that are based on some rationale. This is required for Use Cases that describe how the system may work.

It would also be smart to reuse what is already accumulated in other areas. And if we try to apply experience that has been accumulated in cognitive and computer sciences and software and computer industries, we shall notice some interesting analogies.

Virtual reality and modern computer games become more and more sophisticated, and closer to real life. We are trying to build more and more advanced game engines. But it would be no mistake to state a trivial on the first sight thing: life is also a game. Could our brain use same principles that a sophisticated game engine would be using?

The life game engine needs to drive a core life cycle that consists of perception, cognition, prediction, decision, and action. (See Figure 6) This process is not entirely linear, and there are sub-cycles and feedbacks. For instance, perception and cognition are interdependent. The purpose of cognition is to build a situation model, which is used by the prediction process. Model is created from perceptual information and cognitive models, which also include linguistic models. This is happening with the help of Synthesis – Analysis cycle. The third component of this cycle – Search – is not shown.

Figure 6. Cycles of intelligent life game engine. Please note that a separation between perception and cognition is imaginary and in fact, they form a single multilevel hierarchical system with feedbacks. In this sense, they are perceptual and conceptual levels in the hierarchy with multiple feedbacks between levels rather than separated subsystems. Also, prediction and emotions are shown only between cognition and actions while they form feedback mechanisms on every level.

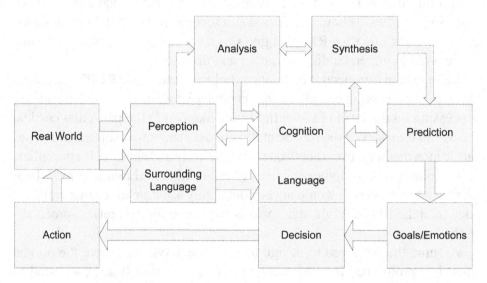

Outcomes of prediction process transform via Goals into Decision. Emotional components play the role of positive or negative feedbacks to generate a Decision upon the cognitive models. Language models are an inseparable part of the cognitive models, and they are shown here as such. The decision turns appropriate Action on, and the cycle repeats.

Indeed the predictions must be accurate and fast. Unlike the computer game, real life doesn't give another chance to replay. So, the path of the processes should be optimal, combining acceptable time with needed quality.

Predictions cannot be made until we have some knowledge. Knowledge can be accumulated, and it is stored in devices that are called "memory." Also, to make fast and accurate decisions, we need to avoid computational complexity. And this means that knowledge/memories have to be organized in a certain way that allows for fast access to relevant information and creation of appropriate models.

Both steps, classification and sequence formation, are necessary to create invariant representations, and each region of cortex does them. The process of forming sequences pays off when an input is ambiguous, and the context of known sequences is used to resolve the ambiguity. The memory of sequences allows not only to resolve ambiguity in the current input but also to predict which input should happen next. A pattern moves back down the hierarchy: stable patterns get "unfolded" into sequences.

In cortical regions, bottom-up classifications and top-down sequences are constantly interacting, changing throughout the life. This is the essence of learning.

So what would be the requirements for such a system?

- Knowledge should be stored in the format that allows for the creation of efficient models. Optimal case would be same representation for perception and cognition, which are part of the loop. In that case, conversions will be avoided.
- Knowledge models format should allow for fast and efficient decision making.
- Knowledge should be ordered in some optimal way, which allows for quick access.
- Knowledge models should reflect the same essential structure and order that exists in the real world.
- Knowledge models should be represented in some invariant abstract form. It is impossible to carry in memory each concrete object or event except an essential one that system observes/faces to regularly.

Let's see what informational structures meet those requirements.

- The structure must contain elements that allow for a quick decision.
  - The decision means a certainty. The uncertain decision is ineffective, and simply makes no sense, turning into a random choice.
  - There must be a mechanism for converting uncertainty into certainty.
  - And model structures should contain preferably elements that are certain, those avoiding many conversions from uncertainty to certainty, wherever possible.
- The structure must be relational.
  - The relation is a constraint that reduces the risk of combinatorial explosion.
  - Relation is a natural invariant, and it captures what consistently occur together

- ◦   Relation captures essential properties of the World, such as spatial, timing, cause and effect, etc
  - ◦   We perceive the World as a nested hierarchical, relational structure.
- The structure must be hierarchical and nested.
  - ◦   In that case, complexity reduced to a particular level.
  - ◦   This also allows for using context and fast and efficient navigation and search in every direction.
  - ◦   It also compresses information in the most efficient way.
  - ◦   Large-scale relationships stored at the top of the hierarchy, and small-scale relationships stored toward the bottom.
- The model structures should have effective mechanisms for maintaining knowledge base.
  - ◦   Methods by which it learns should naturally discover the hierarchical relationships in the world.
  - ◦   This includes not only learning from the input stream but also an automatic derivation of knowledge models.

Unlike a camera's memory, the brain remembers the world as it is, not as it appears. When human think about the world, they recall sequences of patterns that correspond to the way the objects in the world are and how they behave, not how they appear through any particular sense at any point in time. The sequences by which they experience objects in the world reflect the invariant structure of the world itself.

The volume of stored knowledge can be pretty large. But human can only experience a subset of the world at any moment in time. And a person can process only a limited amount of relevant information in a sequential order. This is a limitation of the human processing system, and it is well known that a regular person can actually control just a few points/concepts in their mind at the same time. For more, a crew is needed. What if a computer system could control more points than an average human does?

From the first sight, looks like human brain fights with computational complexity. This is true, but only partially. The processing capability limited with resources that are needed to concentrate on the problem. The recourses that activate relevant information are limited, and focus of attention lost. If someone is tired and cannot concentrate, the problem cannot be solved.

Also, humans are helpless in their intelligent tasks not only without language but also without external carriers like as paper in the past and the computers now. This is a limitation of human memory mechanisms that requires external carriers for expressing models as visuals or language constructs.

Just imagine what humanity could achieve if there is nothing to write or draw on. Human will turn back into savages. But computers will not need paper in case of active semiotic representation.

We will show how such Semiotics systems possess capabilities to represent any knowledge in a unified format. And if making them active, implementing certain methods and architecture, they can not only learn but also derive knowledge, automatically order it, and build new relevant prediction models.

The order is a necessary feature of an active knowledge system. The crucial point is that order is reflected by topology. If we need to organize anything in order, we need to create a topology.

The first degree of order is when some elements are combined into a set. Set is an unordered collection of items. How can elements be chosen for the set? Usually, such a selection process has certain criteria. It might be some structural or functional features.

The definition of structural features is broad to include anything that can be shown as a static permanent feature, would it be an element, quality, level in the hierarchy, part of the relational structure, etc. So does the definition of a functional feature that includes every dynamic feature, process, etc. that change in time.

In this case, a set represents the class. And the process of creation such a set is called a generalization. However, in a more generic case, the process of creating a set of the elements does not require any criteria. It would be just enough to place the items in some space that separates those elements of the set from the rest of the world.

How do the elements of the set look like? Obviously, the traditional representation is Venn diagram, when elements are spatially included in the set. How would it work for the cortical areas? The situation depicted in the diagram. Topology 1 may have place only when wiring of cortical areas is done in the way that similar things are stored in close proximity. But same can be achieved with Hierarchical Topology 2 (See Figure 7)

Here we need to introduce a concept of Space. Space is an entity that limits some phenomena within some bounds. In a more narrow sense, space may contain some entities or their symbols, and their relations, separating them from the others. A spatial model of a Space would be a distributed continuous area. However, in a general case, Space is not necessarily continuous, but it is connected, and it is possible to get from one place to another one within the same space without leaving its boundaries.

Figure 7. Hierarchical topological representation of semiotics. Each entity can have its symbol that stands for this entity as of a single unit in other levels or spaces. Such symbols can be generated (or derived) automatically. Symbols are implicit, and they do not require explicit naming that is shown in the figure only for better illustration. Topologies 1 and 2 are equivalent. Topology 1 represents a distributed set or an alphabet of distributed entities A, B, and C that resides in a proximity in some space D. Same can be achieved in a Hierarchical Topology 2, where symbols a, b, and c representing distributed entities A, B, and C, respectively, reside in a space D, which is on the above level of hierarchy. The overall connectedness is the same. But topology 2 is more generic because spaces that represent entities A, B, and C can be now remote, and they are linked via their symbols residing in a space D.

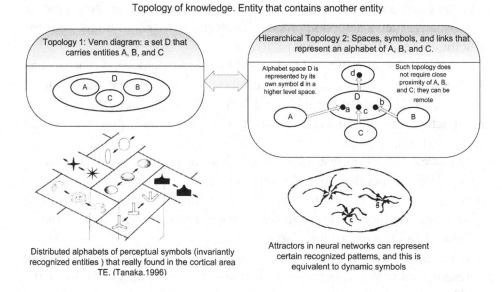

Certainty or possibility can be equivalent to some energy. Points of space can have some possibility/certainty above null that bounded phenomena reside within its borders. Outside of those borders, the possibility/certainty is 0.

In this sense, it is close to the concept of Set, which is an entity that includes other entities. A set can be considered as a kind of the Space.

A symbol is something that denotes an entity and can stand for it in other places. A symbol is equivalent to a recognized entity with certainty closed to 100%. The best representation of a 100% certain value is a crisp number on a linear axis or a point in some distributed area. Energy reaches its maximum at that point.

A set that carries symbols is called an Alphabet. This is a known fact that such Alphabets are found in the cortical area TE (or IT).

Space can also carry relations between the entities or symbols that are equivalent to the entities. Therefore, Space becomes a pattern itself, and it can be recognized as a distinctive entity. Space can also have its symbol, representing this space in the other levels. (See Figure 7)

Processes of generalization and classification are natural with such hierarchical topological representation. Figure 8 shows their equivalence with Venn diagrams.

Systems are natural phenomena, but this is also the way how we order and structure the information about the real world in our efforts to predict things. When we have a system model, there is an order between the elements of system. And this allows us to understand and control the situation.

Figure 8. Generalization and classification in the hierarchical semiotic topology. Processes of generalization and classification can be represented by topologies. As we can see, the topology 2 with distributed entities (Venn diagram) can be equivalent to the hierarchical topology 1. The difference between generalization and classification is the existence of a classifier a that is common to all entities B, C, and D that form class A. Generalization does not require such a classifier. In general case, it also does not require proximity of entities B, C, and D, and it may occur for any remote entities if their activation coincides in time.

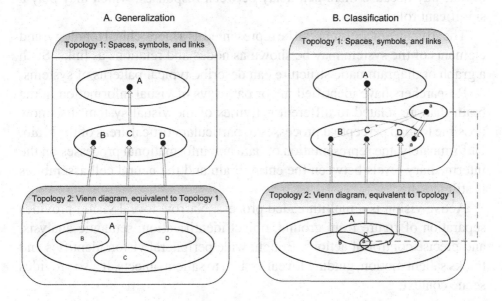

Therefore, the goal of human knowledge is to build a system model that we can use at least for prediction. A system has components, structure, processes, and in some cases goals. Our mental models are systematic models, and same refers to language.

Our knowledge system tries to make things in a systematic way at least partially. There is the logic of interaction between elements, and this logic is applicable for analysis and synthesis of system models.

A system has a set of elements that represent some entities. An entity can be another subsystem, and the entire structure becomes nested. And elements of the system are bound into a coherent structure with relationships between the elements.

Quantitative system models that are described by differential equations are most well known. But there are also qualitative system models that capture cause-effect logics, and they are most close to language and cognitive models that we human use in our everyday decision making.

The relationship can be static (or spatial), and such relationship is usually shown as a bidirectional link. The relationship can be dynamic (or temporal), and such relationship is generally shown as a unidirectional link. A temporal link indicates the order in the sequence. Such a relation usually describes a process or a causal relationship.

Sometimes a feedback exists between the elements, and such interrelationship is also shown as a bidirectional link. But in this case, there are two separate unidirectional links, and it would be better to have them in that way because there is a delay between responses, which may play a significant role.

The structure of a system can be represented as a hierarchical topology, and elements of the system may be shown as nodes and relations as links. Such a graph or diagrammatic structure can describe typical patterns of systems.

Researchers have identified major pathways of visual information in the brain that are related to different activities of the visual system. It is now possible to map perceptual processes to particular cortical areas of the brain. Unfortunately, the representation of data and informational processes on the intermediary levels between the entire brain and the neural cell assemblies is still lacking.

Active vision is a multithreaded process. Narrow foveal vision provides separation of figure from ground, object identification, semantic analysis, and precise control of actions. Rough, wide peripheral vision identifies and tracks salient motion, guiding foveal system to salient objects. It also provides scene context.

In the brain, spatial information hierarchically converts from quantities to qualities, from qualities to objects, from objects to spatial situations. Temporal perceptual information transforms from changes to actions, from actions and objects to events, from events to cause & effect relationships, and from cause & effect relationships to algorithms and scenarios. There are also feedback projections. If all of this is laid out on paper, the result is a schema called "The Informational Pathway."

Natural image processing requires a conversion of images into relational Network-Symbolic structures, instead of precise computations of 3-D models of visual scenes. Primary visual areas convert visual information into "granular" symbolic form. Objects with rigid bodies and other stable systems have coherent relational structures. Hierarchical compression and other transformations in the higher cortical areas derive more abstract structures, which allow recognizing a particular structure as an exemplar of class.

Representation of images as Network-Symbolic structures solves the image "understanding" problems. Humans understand color, sizes, distances, etc. without accurate computations. A Symbolic/Model Space is used as a "measuring device." In the case of Color, the scale of light waves is quantified by fuzzy sets of rainbow colors. The point in the qualitative part represents a symbol of color. References, or links, to such implicit symbols are enough or "understanding" of a basic set of colors.

Another symbolic space produces Linear Scale Device if the axis is quantified by the same fuzzy sets. Hierarchical connections between such linear devices create a layered grid-like structure. Interconnections between layers create another space, which can be considered as a Logarithmic Scale Device. The combination of both devices creates a Size Measuring Device, which is a qualitative analog of a number system.

The vision system, equipped with a set of Color and Size Measuring symbolic devices, can use qualitative values, obtained from such devices, for logical operations. This way such system "understands" color and proportions. Orientation also can be represented in a symbolic form and used in logical operations, if there is a symbolic space, which quantifies a continuous set of directional angles into a finite set of sections.

More complex structures, like geons, can also be represented as patterns with their symbols in Symbolic Spaces.

In the Network-Symbolic systems, both systematic structural methods and neural/statistical methods are parts of a single mechanism. A feedback link can provide supervised learning. The pattern can be recognized by neural or statistical mechanisms. But if it cannot be recognized, the combination of parts or relative location provides a context hypothesis, identifying a symbol of the candidate object via mechanisms of systematic models.

If a distinctively different combination of parts led to the recognition of the same object, then another closure link to the same symbol will appear in the system. A system of such closures, linked to the symbol of the same object, can provide recognition of an object from multiple views without any computations of its 3-D model.

Such Network-Symbolic transformations handle patterns repeated in space equally well as the patterns repeated in time. The mysterious "Gestalts" mechanisms explicitly appear to be hierarchical relational grouping effects, obtained via multilevel graph transformations of primary relational structures of the images.

As it was shown in the generalization example on the previous Figure 8, a Space on the new hierarchical level can carry a set of symbols of entities from the previous level that is activated simultaneously or in some sequence. In the same way, it can carry a set of relations between entities, would it be bidirectional (spatial) or unidirectional (temporal) ones. This represents a structure of the system, which is the most general informational category, and a basis of information models. This situation is shown on Figure 9.

As we can see from Figure 10, any subsystem can be placed inside its Space, and it can have its symbol. That symbol will denote this entity on the

Figure 9. Systematic information in the brain and its topological representation

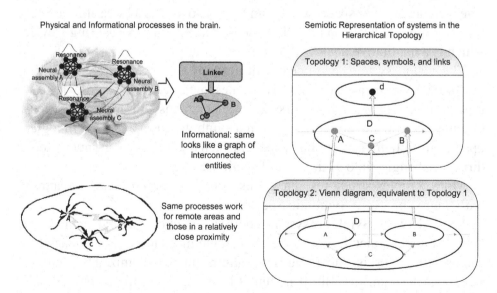

Figure 10. An example of topology of a hierarchical system represented in certainty dimension with implicit symbols

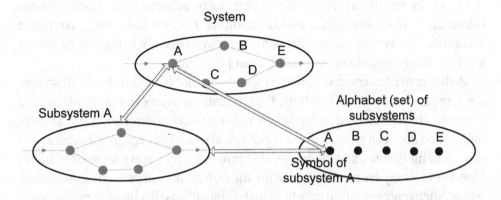

upper level of hierarchy or in any other places, and this significantly helps to remove redundancy and reduce computational complexity.

Similar symbols may be gathered in some proximity space where they create a set or an alphabet. In that alphabet, a symbol of subsystem uniquely identifies such a subsystem. The symbol is an outcome of the recognition, which selects between the entities.

The link between the subsystem and its symbol may work in either direction. Using this link, when the symbol is known, the space with subsystem can be found, and details identified. Context and top-down algorithms work in the same way. (See Figure 10)

REPRESENTING SYSTEMS AND KNOWLEDGE AS DIAGRAMS

We agree that brain describes the world order. How does it do it? Is this representation entirely relies on the physiology of neurons? Or, the mathematical model is independent of the biology? If yes, it can be modeled in any environment that follows certain principles.

A diagram reflects system topology, where elements and processes are denoted by some symbols. When a diagram is processed visually, such image is capable of directly creating a mental model of the system with minimal derivations. In the software and system architecture disciplines, we are working with diagrams a lot, and they nicely represent our knowledge about systems.

Diagrams can substantially simplify understanding of the presented topics. It exactly reflects the topological model of represented knowledge. Language models may require at least a few sentences to achieve same results where information from sentences will be combined into a coherent, systematic mental model. We also know that some early systems of writing like Egyptian were of diagrammatic nature rather than phonetics.

A diagram uses some distributed spaces, symbols, and links. If all spaces are represented by their symbols, the diagram converts into a graph, where symbols are represented by nodes. A point depicts node. But as we already mentioned above, a point is also a topological model of certainty, because it is crisp, unambiguous, and all energy that represents certainty focused in there. Uncertainty may be represented with some distribution or some continuous space. Such representation may help in the algorithms that increasing certainty to find needed information.

Figure 11 shows basic concepts of such topological semiotic representation. A distributed Space represents an entity. Space may be linked to its Symbol. Entity, where all elements are unique but not ordered, is a Set (or an Alphabet). If members are allowed to appear more than once, this is a Multiset (or Bag). A Space with its contents can be split into smaller spaces (separation) or merged with other spaces and their contents (blending).

Order starts appearing when relations of different types are introduced between the elements. Relations exist in the form of links, and they could be bidirectional (spatial), unidirectional (temporal). They can be static (stable for saved structures) or dynamic (unstable for derived structures that exist only for some time during the derivation process). We also may add there a rapid association link that involuntary links together two simultaneously or sequentially activated entities or symbols.

Figure 11. Basic topological concepts of semiotics that represent knowledge in certainty dimension

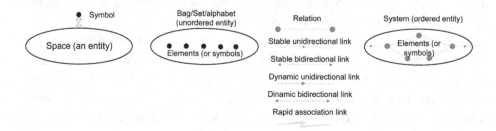

The introduction of relations helps to reduce combinatorial and computational complexities. A relation may also be denoted by its implicit symbol.

The concept of implicit symbols and implicit labeling is explained in Figure 12. It is well known that there is no homunculus in the brain nor there are explicit symbols, which are shown on the figure just to demonstrate the concept of labeling. So how do we obtain meanings? The answer is simple and obvious: our symbols are nodes of the entire knowledge network, and they denote patterns that are learned or derived within that knowledge network. Some symbols can come from the perception processes, and they denote a recognized perceptual pattern of an object or sequence. This is why in the traditional semiotics the concepts of symbol, sign, and icon are hard to distinguish.

We are, however, making a step above the traditional semiotics. In our topological representation, a symbol means a node in the knowledge network that stands for a recognized pattern. This may work in the same way for perceptual and conceptual information.

Conceptual information is more abstract than perceptual one, and it is not linked so much close to real world phenomena. In our semiotic model, concepts

Figure 12. Implicit labeling

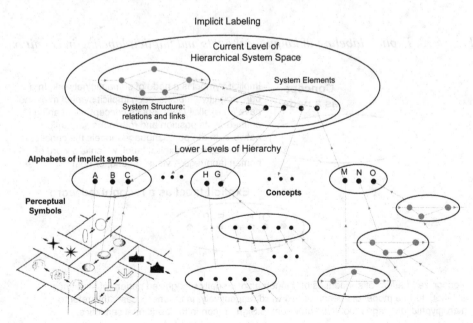

appear as nodes in the knowledge network. It is often that a new concept has no equivalent in the human language. There are some common categories that exist in different languages that denote most common concepts of the models. These are verbs (processes), nouns (entities), adjectives (features), etc.

So how may all of this look from the semiotics topology standpoint? How does a systematic hierarchical model look like from the informational standpoint? How does this correspond to the brain models? And what do we need to build a systematic hierarchical model?

Figure 13 shows one level of the hierarchy of such a model. As we pointed before, there are no explicit symbols in the model on Figure.13. Almost all existing computer models of knowledge and intelligence are based on linguistic models. Linguistic information is simply hard coded in their models. Although such a representation has many advantages, all these models suffer from one major flaw, which severely restricts their practical usage. They are limited to what is typed in, and they can hardly derive a new knowledge. This is a representation problem.

From the informational standpoint, our model has to carry a system, which comprises of system elements and their relations. The structure is a relationally ordered entity. But what denotes the nodes of the structure that are elements of the system for the current level? On the Figure 14 we see a set of elements. And the elements of this set are implicit symbols. This is an imaginary operation for the real cortical structures, where implicit symbols

Figure 13. Explicit labeling in language models and implicit labeling in cognition

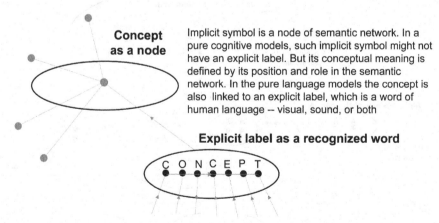

Concept as a node

Implicit symbol is a node of semantic network. In a pure cognitive models, such implicit symbol might not have an explicit label. But its conceptual meaning is defined by its position and role in the semantic network. In the pure language models the concept is also linked to an explicit label, which is a word of human language -- visual, sound, or both

Explicit label as a recognized word

C O N C E P T

Recognized pattern of sequences of phonemes or visually recognized pattern of sequence of letters form a model of speech or text word respectively. In a general case, this refer to hieroglyphic languages too. It is equivalent to Sign or Icon in the traditional semiotics.

Figure 14. Synthesis of diagrammatic semiotic models by analogy

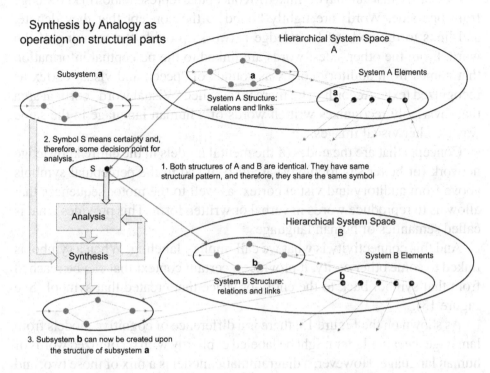

simply may be connected to the nodes via some activation channels. But it doesn't change anything in the model. For artificial computer representation, these could be pointers, references, or direct copies of symbols in those cases where the original ones can be easily found in the alphabet where this symbol is defined.

If the same patterns exist anywhere else, they should be linked to the same symbol. In that case, all patterns of the same kind can always be replaced on the top level with their symbol. And Space that carries this information will be much more compact, certain, and can represent and understand the structure that exists between connected patterns. Such phenomenon is called hierarchical compression. This helps the brain to fight with complexity and redundancy.

Now let's look at the role of language in the entire picture. Knowledge can be transferred with visual diagrams and come from images. But knowledge also can come from texts and speech in the form of human language. We would call language a seventh sense that transfers knowledge.

Obviously, that language is linked to conceptual representation of knowledge from one side. Words are tightly bound to the concept that they denote, and links to the node of knowledge networks provide the meaning of the word. From the other sides, words are linked to the perceptual information that comes from auditory cortex as sounds of speech and visual cortex as recognized texts. According to, there is so-called "Visual word" cortical area that invariably recognizes written words of a human language in the same way as other visual images.

Concepts that are the nodes of the mental models in the entire knowledge network (or better say topology) are also linked to the perceptual symbols above from auditory and visual cortex, as well to the motor sequences that allow us to reproduce words in verbal or written form. This provides what is called semantics of human language.

And this connectivity is what we call implicit labeling. When a symbol is linked to some other entity, it provides a certain context that can be reached from that symbol back to the entity or space that created that symbol (See Figure 13).

As shown on the Figure 13, there is a difference of cognitive models from language, because latter might be labeled explicitly with recognized words of human language. However, a diagrammatic model is a mix of those two, and it allows for operations that lead to creation new spaces and symbols on the fly. In this sense, it is understandable (interpretable) by the system that has game engine build in. But it is not necessarily entirely expressible in human language. And human use drawings in such cases.

The mixed diagrammatic nature of systematic, intelligent models is another reason why linguistic models of intelligence failed to meet the expectations.

What advantages can we get from this representation?

It allows for unified operations on the structural part separately from the context of its elements. Analogy and metaphors were always a mystery for models that are based on language and formal logics. Figure 14 shows them as operations on the structural part.

Analogy requires some basis. Human usually based analogy on some similarity. This similarity may be expressed nicely regarding systematic structural models. If the structure of systems is similar, we may expect a similar behavior. So if we do synthesis, then we can design a particular system B, using original system An as a prototype. The challenge for our case is that intelligent system needs doing this without human intervention. So it needs to "understand" somehow that the similarity exists. This is an unsolvable problem for the hard coded linguistic models. But for our representation, this is a regular operation upon structural parts that leads to the derivation of a symbol upon the recognition of similarity. A symbol is also a decision point that can be used by synthesis- analysis cycle.

In the same way, topological representation allows for conceptual blending of a few models into one consistent, systematic model (See Figure 15), or an easy splitting into a few ones if needed.

The operations above were always challenging for the traditional linguistic models. And this part of intelligence lacked in such systems, leaving them very restricted in their capabilities to some logical operations and to what is hard coded (literally typed in) there. Not surprisingly, that expert systems mainstream ended in fiasco.

Also, topological semiotic representation provides significant hierarchical compression, because similar parts can be replaced with their symbols. It also provides self-describing codes, which help intelligent system to understand

Figure 15. The operation of conceptual blending is about merging spaces. In some cases, we may need opposite operation of splitting spaces to reduce computational complexity.

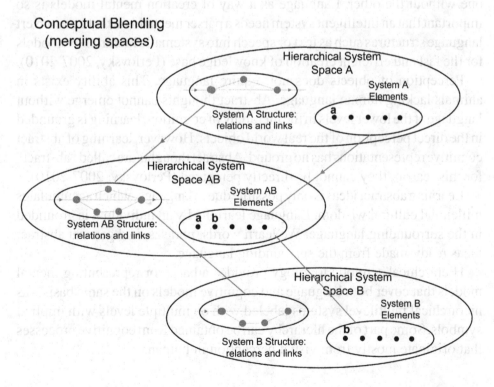

73

how the system is organized and function in the context of its relationship with other concepts and systems on multiple levels.

It is important to mention that symbols can be learned as result of the recognition process. But they also can be derived as result of some automatic graph transformation. Such transformations are accountable for proofs, solving mathematical problems. Interestingly, but it appeared that a mystical "invention" process could also be formalized as a set of diagrammatic operations, as it was shown in the TRIZ (or TIPS - Theory of Invention Problems Solving) system. (Altshuller, 1999).

None of the existing linguistic models can do that. Their representations allow for understanding by a human. But once a human is in the loop, they can do it better.

REPRESENTING COGNITION IN THE HIERARCHICAL SEMIOTIC TOPOLOGY

Our criticism of existing linguistic models does not imply neglect of language. Language and cognition are so closely related that it's hard to imagine what one without the other. Language as a way of creation mental models is so important that an intelligent system needs a parser mechanism that can convert language structures such as text or speech into systematic hierarchical models for the fast and efficient creation of knowledge base (Perlovsky, 2007-2010).

Perception of objects does not require language. This ability exists in animals lacking human language. Abstract thoughts cannot emerge without language at the lower levels in the hierarchy of cognition, learning is grounded in the direct perception of the real world objects. However, learning of abstract cognitive representations has no ground. Abstract thoughts are called "abstract" for this reason; they cannot be directly perceived (Perlovsky, 2007-2010).

Learning abstract ideas is only possible due to language, which accumulates millennial cultural wisdom. Language learning by an individual is grounded in the surrounding language. We learn words, phrases, and general abstract ideas ready-made from the surrounding language.

Hierarchical semiotic topology provides a basis for representing mental models that cover both language and cognitive models on the same basis – as hierarchical multilevel systems labeled with on multiple levels with implicit symbols. Some part of the hierarchy can be obtained from cognitive processes that originate mostly from visual perception in human.

Same representation is repeated at every hierarchical level, yet the meaning of is different at every level. At lower levels, implicit symbols denote sensor features and objects in the cognitive parts of the hierarchy, and these symbols are labeled with corresponding words in the language part.

Symbols higher up in the hierarchy denote more abstract mental models of objects, situations, abstract ideas, interactions, and processes. In the same way, they are labeled with corresponding words where such words exist for those concepts.

The connections between the implicit symbols and linguistic labels are promptly established with a Pavlovian reflex that seems to be inborn. In this way, language and cognitive contents are always staying connected.

Human learning of cognitive models continues through the lifetime and is guided by language. Abstract concepts form systematic models that are derived from human language and not learned from individual experience. And this is what exactly distinct human from animals.

Understanding may not be reduced to a memory recall only. Any solution to a practical problem requires a systematic model, which can be used for in the life game engine. And human life engine is much better than animal ones in solving practical tasks mostly because a human can learn needed models from the language.

Syntactic structures possess a challenge. People are not talking or reading with words only. Words are wrapped into sentences that are real units of knowledge transfer. And sentences form texts that carry knowledge.

It is evident that both sentence and text provide the higher level context that helps to fight ambiguity. But how could it happen? The answer is that context is a mental conceptual model that comes from the story or stories that are contained in the text. Therefore, linguistic construct in the syntactic form is helping us in building systematic mental models. And when we are coming back from mental models, we are creating linguistic constructs out of our mental models.

A person may be bilingual, and their native language constructs might differ very significantly. Anyway, the meaning, which is a systematic conceptual model, remains the same in the head of the person, and it is independent of syntax existing in different languages.

Figure 16 shows an idea of the linguistic parser that is based on parallel hierarchies of cognition and language. Limitations of existing speech recognition systems are well known. They are usually based on HMM models that allow for prediction of certain sound sequences those improving overall recognition rate.

Figure 16. constructing multilevel semiotic models from the human language constructs using parallel hierarchies of cognition and language

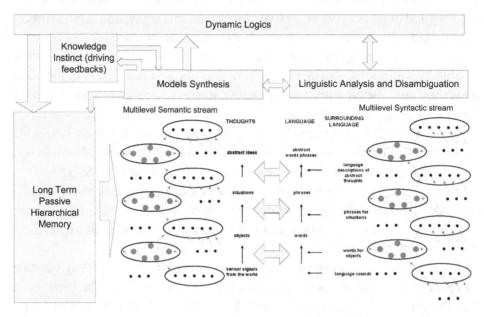

But even if such system would be able to reach 100% accuracy, a significant problem of such systems is that they are not intelligent. Except for some very simple cases that can be formalized, most of the situations that people are calling about require a human operator. This may somehow reduce load, but severely restricts the practical application of speech recognition. This somewhat improves the situation in the calling centers but does not change it drastically.

In case, when system possesses more intelligence, the situation would be different. First of all, it would significantly improve recognition outcomes, which is now far from perfect. It is well known that accurate recognition requires top level context. And it is based on an understanding of the situation, because in many cases ambiguous outcomes of perception process might be interpreted differently, depending on the situation.

This context may be more accurately provided from semantic models that are responsible for meaning. And as we have shown above, semantic models are upper levels of more generic semiotic models that start from the perceived object features.

But even for cases when a 100% accuracy of recognition is achieved, the problem of understanding human language was never solved. For us the solution is a dynamic construction of systematic hierarchical semiotic models from human language.

Figure 16 shows a system that solves this problem using a dual hierarchy of language and cognition. This model explains several aspects of the interaction between semantic and syntax of the language that seems unexplainable otherwise.

The system does a synthesis of hierarchical multilevel systematic semiotic models in the semantic stream, using following two major input streams:

- Multilevel syntactic stream that carries parsed sentences and phrases from written text or speech.
- Long term passive hierarchical memory that already contains learned or derived models.

Syntactic models help to parse human language text into certain predefined constructs. These model constructs are mapped to corresponding models constructs of the semantic stream due to the parallel hierarchy of cognition and language.

Synthesis process uses information extracted by analysis of syntactic models above as well as semantic models that are extracted from long term memory. The problem of matching concepts and models to human language is the problem of explicit labeling, which was previously described in this book. This problem is nicely addressed with the powerful mechanism of Dynamic Logic (DL). Dynamic Logic is also used for extracting relevant information from long-term passive hierarchical memory. This is shown on Figure 16.

The cognitive grammar of Langacker (2008) is based on the idea that language is underlined with some perceptual constructs. Langacker (2008) provides his set of schematic diagrams that depict such perceptual processes.

REFERENCES

Altshuller, G. (1999). *The Innovation Algorithm: TRIZ, systematic innovation, and technical creativity*. Worcester, MA: Technical Innovation Center.

Hebb, D. O. (1949). *The Organization of Behavior*. New York: Wiley & Sons.

Kuvich, G. (2003). Reduction of computational complexity in the image/video understanding systems with active vision. *Proceedings SPIE, 5267*, 125-136.

Kuvich, G. (2004). Image/video understanding systems based on network-symbolic models and active vision. *Proceedings SPIE, 5438*, 1-12. doi:10.1117/12.541271

Kuvich, G. (2005). Perception system with scene understanding capabilities upon network-symbolic models for intelligent tactical behavior of mobile robots in real-world environments. *Proceedings of the SPIE*, 6006. doi:10.1117/12.630300

Kuvich, G. (2005). Automatic target detection and identification with a scene understanding system based on network-symbolic models. *Proceedings SPIE, 5807*, 409-422. doi:10.1117/12.603026

Langacker, R. (2008). *Cognitive Grammar*. Oxford University Press. doi:10.1093/acprof:oso/9780195331967.001.0001

Marr, D. (1982). *Vision*. New York: W.H.Freeman.

MPEG-7. (2017). In *Wikipedia*. Retrieved 2017 from https://en.wikipedia.org/wiki/MPEG-7

Pavlov, I. P. (1927). *Conditioned Reflexes: An Investigation of the Physiological Activity of the Cerebral Cortex* (G. V. Anrep, Trans. & Ed.). London: Oxford University Press.

Perlovsky, L. I. (2007). Neural Networks, Fuzzy Models and Dynamic Logic. In R. Köhler & A. Mehler (Eds.), Aspects of Automatic Text Analysis (pp. 363-386). Springer.

Perlovsky, L. I., & Ilin, R. (2010). Neurally and Mathematically Motivated Architecture for Language and Thought. *The Open Neuroimaging Journal, 4*, 70–80. doi:10.2174/1874440001004020070 PMID:21673788

Sowa, J. (2000) Knowledge Representation. Brooks/Cole.

Chapter 3
Driving Mechanisms and Patterns

ABSTRACT

This chapter explains role of positive and negative feedback mechanisms that are similar to emotions, and can drive processes to reach goals.

INTRODUCTION

The top structures of our knowledge network describe learned situations and experience. We can create new models of other structures spontaneously. To create or derive new situational models and scenarios, the old models and scenarios must be split into smaller models. Language provides this opportunity, breaking everything into a set of smaller structures – sentences. In a certain order, they create a larger complete network model that describes a new situation, or scenario.

A simple sentence carries an observation that is called "fact." The observed facts have a very high degree of certainty because it is observed. There are also cause and effect links when events are coming together, and existing of one observation may lead to anticipation of the linked one. Such related observations also have a high degree of certainty because they are observed together as cause and effect.

Spatial knowledge is represented by specifying qualitative relationships of and between spatial entities. Different kinds of spatial relationships representing different aspects of space: size, distance, orientation, shape, etc.

DOI: 10.4018/978-1-5225-2431-1.ch003

Spatial relationships are universal, and they describe how observed distinct entities may locate in space about each other. For instance, there are eight spatial relations for regions on the planar surface that are the basis for the Region Connected Calculus (RCC-8), depicted in Figure 1. The Region Connection Calculus (RCC) by Randell, Cui, and Cohn (1992) is the best-known approach to qualitative spatial representation.

Qualitative spatial representation is intended to describe relationships between spatial entities such as regions or points of a particular space, for instance, of a two- or three-dimensional Euclidean space. Topology offers a theory of space by categorizing different kinds of spaces, so-called topological spaces, according to different properties. And topology fits well to the case which does not depend on a 2 or 3-dimensional space but can be applied to a more general notion of space, which is the case here.

The topology may include the concept of a topological space; different kinds of regions such as open/closed; different parts of regions such as the

Figure 1. Fundamental spatial relationships between planar regions that comprise RCC-8

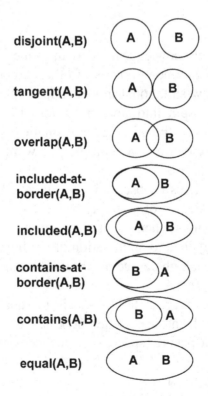

interior, the exterior and the boundary of a region, as well as neighborhoods, neighborhood systems, and different kinds of points. These concepts are very basic and can be found in this or a similar form in any book on general topology or point-set topology.

Such relations represent not only spatial schema. But in a primary sense, they represent a particular logical schema. Regions may represent restricted areas that have certain information phenomena included, while outside of those areas such phenomena do not exist. This is pretty much the concept of Space, which was introduced earlier.

We should mention that this boundary is purely imaginary, and is not limited to a 2D or any n-dimensional spatiality. Space may include informational phenomena even in very remote areas. The spatial RCC-8 illustration is just a very vivid private case, which is very easy to understand and take as an analogy.

Such relations also serve as an illustration for some logical phenomena. For instance, the Overlay is frequently used for illustrating logics, such as for example Venn Diagrams. Logical AND and OR are usually perfectly illustrated with some Venn or Euler diagrams.

It is pretty easy to take two Symbolic or Model Spaces and to check them for the common elements or patterns. If such common elements or patterns do exist, they form AND. On the diagram, it is an intersection. The union of both Spaces makes logical OR.

However, such models are artificial. We can conclude that they can be handled on the level of their symbols. Assume that we have two spaces: A and B, both represented with their symbols a and b on the next level of the hierarchy. Assume that there is a standard part of them, which can be identified with patterns matching. It appears to be either a subset or a subsystem. Such a common element may have its own symbol C, which will stand for such a subset or a subsystem. This symbol also may denote $A \cap B$.

Spaces A and B can be spatially remote but have same common part.

Another type of relations may be Equivalence relations. What happened, in this case, is that common parts set up an Equivalence relationship, which has its symbol. And this symbol can substitute for the common part.

The common part can be moved into a separate space with its symbol. Now the remaining parts from A and B will be connected directly to this new space, and the entire picture will look like spatially linked to the common part.

In this way, we can achieve a high degree of topological compression. Commonalities will be replaced with their symbol, which refers to the common part. This may work in a topological model. But how does this work for the real brain on the cortical level?

I believe that it works in the same way there. As we know from Hawkins, the sequence of patterns has its name on the next level. This "name" is an activation coming to the next level. In the certainty dimension, it is equivalent to Symbol regarding this work.

Most probably, the mechanism is following. The incoming patterns are subject to recognition. When nothing similar is found, a new pattern is created. The resulting pattern or sub-pattern is subject to recognition. So on the next level, such piece of information is denoted with its symbol, and this symbol is substituted for the entire pattern. In this way, we know that certain parts of the image are merely the same patterns, like this happen for instance with textures.

For that, we should admit that this process must be sequential. And here we may need to define temporal relationships. Time is just a speed of processes that are happening in space. But it convenient to reason about time, when using time points and representing the possible relationships between them.

Providing temporal relations with formal semantics is much easier than it is for spatial ones. Temporal entities are either are time points or time intervals which can be represented by their endpoints. Temporal reasoning is mainly reasoning about ordered points, no matter what aspects of temporal entities are taken into account, order, distance, extension.

That leads to the concept of the time interval. Thirteen base relations of Allen's interval algebra (1983) relations are applicable to time intervals. (See Figure 2)

Topological relationships are those relationships that are invariant on continuous transformations of the underlying space: "C is inside D," "B overlaps D," or "C touches E" are examples of topological relationships.

Qualitative reasoning is an approach for dealing with knowledge information in certainty dimension, those avoiding numerical calculations. Knowledge is represented by limited set of qualitative relationships between entities or qualitative categories of numerical values

Let's discuss a notion of set. Set is least ordered information category. It has elements that comprise the alphabet of the set. In mathematical extensional notation elements of the set are listed in curly brackets, like for instance {2, 6}. The set {2, 6, 6, 2} still means the same {2, 6}. So only unique elements are counted in the set, which resembles the notion of an alphabet.

From the Cognitive Semiotics point of view, the elements of an alphabet are Symbols that stand for distinct patterns. Symbols gathered in the set or

Figure 2. Temporal relations

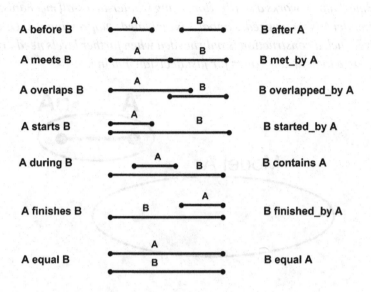

alphabet are actually distinctive, because recognition of an item of the alphabet automatically means that others items were rejected by the recognition. This is pretty much the concept of Exclusive OR logical operation or Winner-Takes-All algorithm in math, and what N. Amosov has called "System of Inhibition and Activation".

Negation is an interesting concept. It was always hard to explain it because negation has multiple sources. Negation means that something has not happened (failed) or anything that does not belongs to an entity.

Spatially or topologically, a negation ¬A can mean everything outside of the Space A. If we want to explicitly represent this situation in the implicit symbols on the top level, it creates a mutually exclusive pair relationship.

We should notice that Symbol on the higher level also means a decision. Another words, activation of symbol A implies that underlying pattern was activated. Therefore, pair A– ¬A is an artificially created Space, which is working on the next decision level for simplification of further decision making process. (See Figure 3)

It is easier to use a signal from the explicit negation node for the further decision process. Otherwise, every time we still have to check where a signal comes from the node that denotes A or not. That would be cumbersome, vs. having an explicit artificially created node symbol for ¬A, which is a ready-made decision that no signal from A.

Figure 3. The concept of negation as an artificially created symbol in some space. The entire mechanism works as a flip-flop, using winner-takes-all mechanism. If the pattern of model A is recognized, symbol A is activated, suppressing ¬A. Otherwise, ¬A is active. Such a construction is only needed when further levels need to use this symbol in some logical constructs for fast decision making.

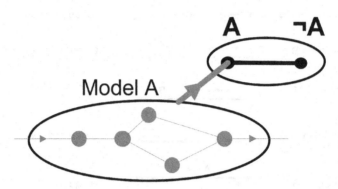

This kind of decision model can be viewed as a semi-ordered set. (See Figure 4) The order appears in the system when relationships between elements are introduced. Let's see what other kinds of semi-ordered sets can be observed in the cortex.

Assume that we have two implicit symbols A and B, activated in a short sequence. Pavlovian reflex mechanism associates these two symbols, creating unidirectional links between them. This means that pattern A may precede pattern B. If this sequence is repeated, the relationship becomes stable. Otherwise, the link disappears with time.

This is how a simple cause-effect relationship established. This link allows deciding where after the pattern we can also expect pattern B. Or, where we observe pattern B, then we could also expect that pattern A preceded it.

Cause – effect relationship is a temporal relation that may be observed in many cases. For instance, for the action – reaction pair.

Now assume that we have linked together multiple cause – effect pairs into some chain. Assume that we have activated the beginning and the end of the chain simultaneously. Then the start of the chain will be linked with the end of the chain in the same way.

Next time we don't need to run through the whole chain. We have a cause – effect relation established between the beginning of the chain and end of the chain. That may significantly accelerate the decision process next time (See Figure 5).

Figure 4. An example of a semi-ordered set with relations between elements

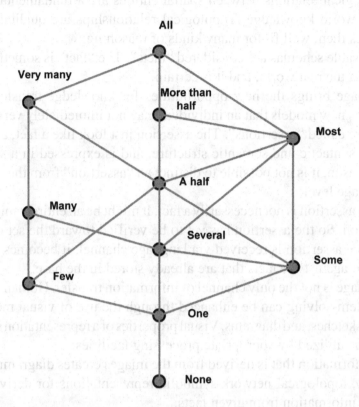

Figure 5. Logical chaining and mathematical proof

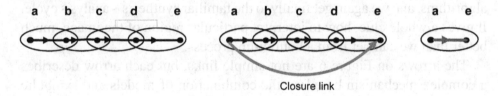

Closure link

The same mechanism drives logical conclusions and mathematical proof. It looks very complicated at first sight. But the underlying phenomena are pretty simple and consist in the chaining of cause – effect links.

All of this comprises so-called commonsense knowledge. The order in which children acquire spatial notions is a topology, orientation, and distance. Other spatial aspects include size, shape, morphology, and motion.

Topological relations between spatial entities are a fundamental part of invariant world knowledge. Topological relationships are qualitative, and that makes them well fit for many kinds of reasoning.

Observable schemas are considered "facts". The "fact" is something that happens in the real world, and it is certain.

Language brings the new opportunities for knowledge transfer. But it also brings new models that an individual may not immediately verify. Such models are called "assertions". The assertion just look like a fact, and it has the same syntactic and semantic structure, and is expressed in a sentence. By that reason, it is not possible to distinct an "assertion" from the "fact" on the language level.

But an assertion is not necessarily a fact. It might be an entirely misleading information. So the assertion has yet to be verified toward the set of stored facts. Once assertion is received via language channel, it becomes possible to check it against the facts that are already stored in the base.

Language is not the only channel of information transfer. Human thinking and problem-solving can be enhanced through the use of visual media like pictures, sketches, and diagrams. Visual properties of a representation structure that can be utilized by appropriate processing facilities.

But information that is derived from the images creates diagrammatic, or better say, topological network-symbolic representations for deriving new pieces of information from given facts.

The top-level structure can provide context hypothesis to the recognition, or in our statement of problem – understanding. That can drive appropriate algorithms, and we again get finally to the familiar synthesis – analysis cycle. It gives a whole clue, how to interpret particular region of the image, much better than we can get from a bottom-up process.

The arrows on Figure 6 are not simple links, but each arrow describes a complex mechanism based on the combination of models and symbolic spaces, their interaction and processes in such environment. The feedback arrows show top-down algorithms of resolving uncertainty and ambiguity in the real images, providing context frames for interpretation. Without it, Image Understanding problem cannot be solved efficiently.

There is a lot of ways to derive top-level structures that can provide context hypothesis to the recognition, or in our statement of problem – understanding. Dual representation naturally combines different methods of machine learning, classification and analogy altogether with induction, deduction and other methods of higher level reasoning within a single framework. The important

Figure 6. A simple example of models and processes of the distributed environment, shown in the certainty dimension

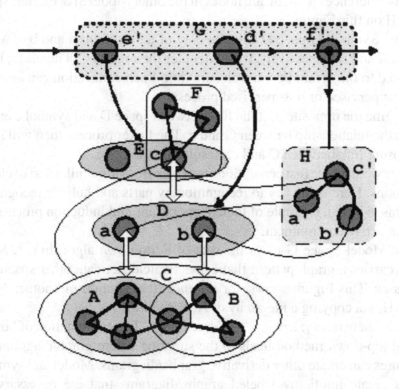

point is that such structural methods can work effectively only within an environment that organically supports such representations.

The system of spaces creates more abstract derivative structures, such as syntactic ones, that act as "measuring devices," or algorithms. Distributed methods give ways of handling with uncertainty, representing it spatially. Dual representation naturally combines methods of classification, analogy, and machine learning, together with induction, deduction and other methods of higher level reasoning within a single framework. Here they are algorithms of transformations of the networks under the laws of search-synthesis-analysis. Logic is simply a way of linking and ordering such networks. (See Figure 6)

On this figure, some Model Spaces A and B create a Model Space C as their union. Spaces A and B have corresponded symbols a and b respectively in the Symbolic Space D. Symbols represent spaces as some units on the next level of the hierarchy.

Model Space C have its symbol c on the Symbolic Space E. Symbols, or links, or references to them, are nodes in the other Model Spaces, like Spaces F and H on this Figure.

If the Symbolic Space D consists only of the symbols a and b of Model Spaces A and B respectively, it also denotes their union C. Therefore, D can be linked to the symbol c via a closure link. Such connection can be set up with a supervised or unsupervised process.

Imagine the opposite. Let the link between space D and symbol c existed before the relationship between C and c. The linker process then will set up the closure link between C and c. Results are the same.

Later we shall see that perception processes are using similar sort of closure operations. Here is the key to recognition by parts and holistic recognition. And this is just an example of logical operations and induction processes in such an active environment.

The Model Space G plays the role of a top-down algorithm. A Model Space carries a graph pattern that can activate/deactivate other spaces and processes. This Figure shows, for instance, the creation of another Model Space H, via copying a hierarchy of A, B, C into.

Such a network system is a "self-operating." The combination of bottom-up and top-down method leads to the situation where graph/diagrammatic structures can create other derivative graphs/diagrams. Model and symbolic spaces create implicitly labeled graphs/diagrams that are necessary and sufficient for the creation of systematic qualitative models. There is no need in "homunculus," or explicit symbolic system here. All possible graph, diagrammatic, and topological operations and transformations are available in such a dual environment. This way the system can build another Model/Symbolic space.

At this point, a few kind words should be said about the traditional Artificial Neural Network models with hidden layers. Theoretically, there are graph algorithms. Graph level is the cortical level, the level of neural assemblies. Therefore, such models can be used for emulation of mechanisms of statistical learning in the information channels between the nodes of our emulated "cortical software" system. Layers of hidden nodes just provide a statistical generalization. Being a part of the entire system, such models look here much more realistic and applicable.

Space is an equivalent to an informational cluster -- a "cortical module." The working unit here is an active space that carries a distributed graph/network model. Spaces, irrelevant at the present moment, are inactive. Some important components and processes are absolute "biologically" necessary for such system of active spaces:

- Linker process
- Attention mechanism

There is a lot of ways to derive top-level structures that can provide context hypothesis to the recognition, or in our statement of problem – understanding. Dual representation naturally combines different methods of machine learning, classification and analogy altogether with induction, deduction and other methods of higher level reasoning within a single framework. However, a description of all possible algorithms simply cannot be given in this book.

A regular Turing machine can work without any "homunculus" because:

1. It has a feedback between the control part and tape memory.
2. Data and programs are represented as the same sequence of symbols in the control section and memory.

Here we have a sort of Distributed, or Spatial Turing Machine (See Figure 7) that differs from a Symbolic Turing Machine:

1. Networks take the place of symbols on tape and control part.
2. Networks are both data and algorithms simultaneously.
3. Networks can rewrite themselves being a memory and the control part simultaneously.

Figure 7. Regular/symbolic Turing machine (left) and spatial Turing machine (right). Networks take the place of symbols and are memory and control part simultaneously.

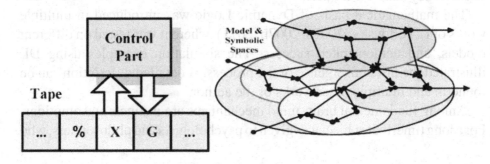

Such a network system is a "self-operational." There is no need in a "homunculus," or an explicit symbolic system here. Graphs/diagrams can create other graphs/diagrams automatically. Processes in such environment have their own goals, and feedback mechanisms drive those processes until the goal is reached.

The long-term passive hierarchical memory is an analog of human memory, which in the same way store multilevel hierarchical models. This memory is huge, and only a relatively small part of it, which is relevant to the current task, is active at one moment of time.

This mathematical problem has often been called combinatorial complexity (CC). The problem is similar to testing all possible combinations of data and models to select the best one in the strong clutter. The number of these combinations even for moderate values is very large. Dynamic Logic (DL) solved this problem using a reasonable number of operations (Perlovsky, 2007a, 2007b, 2011).

DL is inspired by perceptual and cognitive operations of the human mind. Conscious perceptions are preceded by activations of cortex areas storing memories-representations of objects. The DL process proceeds from vague-fuzzy to crisp-logical.

Dynamic Logic addresses abstract compositionality models that are typical for higher level abstract concepts. Relations among compositional parts could be modeled by specific objects-markers.

DL is an extension of fuzzy logic toward including fuzzification and defuzzification operations into logic as its inseparable mechanisms. The fundamental elements of DL are not fuzzy-logic statements or states, but logic-processes. The fundamental process is from vague-fuzzy states to crisp states. These states could be objects, events, contexts, situations, or more abstract concepts. DL overcame computational complexity due to initial vague-fuzzy states of models.

The mathematical basis of Dynamic Logic was introduced in multiple works of L. Perlovsky (2007a, 2007b, 2011), where it was tested on different models, and demonstrated success. The simulation examples using DL illustrated the fast convergence of the process. A detailed description can be found in and multiple other works of the author.

Among fundamental brain-mind mechanisms are instincts and emotions. For a long time, that subject was given to psychologists and philosophers, who focused on most prominent human emotions and instincts, like for instance love, and the subject has been turned into a romantic mystery.

Charles Darwin was one of the first scientists writing about the existence and nature of emotions in animals. Emotional reactions are found in many animals. Feelings of optimism or pessimism have been shown in a wide range of species including rats, dogs, cats, rhesus macaques, sheep, chicks, starlings, pigs, and honey bees. It is widely recognized now animals may feel emotions, and that human emotion evolved from the same mechanisms.

Let's leave aside romantic part of the story, and look at the mechanism of emotions from the practical point of view of the autonomous system. In the natural systems on their physical level, emotions work via complex chemical mechanisms, which are beyond the scope of this book. But if we look at the emotions from the systematic informational level, we can clearly see that all emotions can be categorized into two major polar categories: pleasant and unpleasant.

Pleasant emotion is some feeling that you prefer to maintain as long as possible. It associates with reaching some goal. An example may be emotions associated with a feeling of pleasure.

Unpleasant emotion is some feeling that you prefer to break as soon as possible. It associates with dissatisfaction from unavailability to reaching a goal. Or, you feel yourself in a situation that you should not be, and you need to change it. An example may be emotions associated with a feeling of pain.

According to Encyclopedia Britannica, taxis is a directional response by an organism to a stimulus (Zug, n.d.). This response can be either positive or negative, depending on the perceived stimulus. And we can observe this even in a simplest single cell organism Amoeba. Such a primitive behavior could be anyway compared to complex emotional mechanisms of higher animals because they are similar in their core nature.

In a similar way, all emotions of leaving species from most simple to most complex can be categorized into two basic categories: pleasant and unpleasant. Pleasant emotions require fixation and continuation of the process that makes pleasure. Unpleasant emotions require breaking the process. Therefore, emotions drive processes automatically; while instincts provide the goals for the processes. But in the world of system science, these mechanisms are well known as positive and negative feedback. Negative feedback is maintaining the system in its current state, while positive feedback takes system away from the current state. (See Figure 8)

Figure 8. Emotions as a feedback mechanism

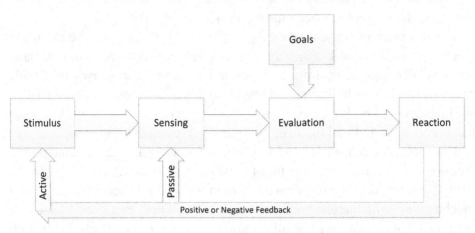

As we can see from the information above, mechanism of emotions from the standpoint of cybernetics plays the role of positive or negative feedback in the process of reaching goals. Such a mechanism is necessary for any self-driving process.

Learning is also a self-driving process. Neuropsychology suggests a few types of learning. But we would like to propose a slightly different classification of learning that is based upon the sources of input information. Perceptual learning obtains input information through perception. Conceptual learning is related to learning abstract information through the language.

These two streams send information into different levels of hierarchical network memory. Perceptual learning converts perceptual information from our senses into meaningful perceptual structures. This process will be detailed further in the consequent chapters.

Where do emotions (and mechanism of feedback) come into play here?

Perception is a dynamic mechanism, and learning there happens constantly. Human learns repeated perceptual information as patterns. But human vision is capable of extracting structures from visual information.

There were significant efforts in conversion image data into meaningful informational structures, and also on the usage of context in the processing of visual information. For instance, Geographic Information Systems (GIS) can adequately address problems with geographic and satellite imagery, because geographic knowledge has been well formalized in the form of maps, and maps can be represented well in digital form.

When it comes to conceptual information, it comes to us in the form of facts. Facts are wrapped into sentences, which are decoded into graph structures that are invariant toward specific flavor of any human language.

Given that the information in the communication channel cannot always be directly verified by human perception, a fact is a logical unit, which can be assigned to a certain degree of trust. That confidence is subjective and based on our feelings toward how well the new factual information model may fit other factual information. If there is a mismatch, the fact is rejected.

In his works, Perlovsky (2006, 2007a, 2007b, 2011, 2012) introduced the concept of Knowledge Instinct (KI) that drives improvement and optimization of mental models-concepts for better correspondence to surrounding objects and events.

Dynamic Logic model of KI inherently involves emotional signals related to satisfaction or dissatisfaction of KI. These emotions are perceived as feelings of harmony or disharmony between personal knowledge and the world or within the knowledge. These are so-called aesthetic emotions, and this mechanism may drive processes on Figure 8.

REFERENCES

Allen, J. F. (1983). Maintaining knowledge about temporal intervals. In *Communications of the ACM*. ACM Press. doi:10.1145/182.358434

Perlovsky, L. I. (2006). Toward physics of the mind: Concepts, emotions, consciousness, and symbols. *Physics of Life Reviews*, *3*(1), 23–55. doi:10.1016/j.plrev.2005.11.003

Perlovsky, L. I. (2007a). Neural Networks, Fuzzy Models and Dynamic Logic. In R. Köhler & A. Mehler (Eds.), *Aspects of Automatic Text Analysis* (pp. 363–386). Springer.

Perlovsky, L. I. (2007b). Neural Dynamic Logic of Consciousness: the Knowledge Instinct. In L. I. Perlovsky & R. Kozma (Eds.), *Neurodynamics of Higher-Level Cognition and Consciousness*. Heidelberg, Germany: Springer Verlag. doi:10.1007/978-3-540-73267-9_5

Perlovsky, L. I. (2012). Brain: Conscious and unconscious mechanisms of cognition, emotions, and language. *Brain Sciences*.

Perlovsky, L. I., Deming, R. W., & Ilin, R. (2011). *Emotional Cognitive Neural Algorithms with Engineering Applications. Dynamic Logic: from vague to crisp*. Heidelberg, Germany: Springer. doi:10.1007/978-3-642-22830-8

Randell, D. A., Cui, Z., & Cohn, A. G. (1992): A spatial logic based on regions and connection. In *Proc. 3rd Int. Conf. on Knowledge Representation and Reasoning* (pp. 165–176). Morgan Kaufmann.

Zug, G. R. (n.d.). Locomotion. *Britannica*. Retrieved May 26, 2017, from https://www.britannica.com/topic/locomotion/Orientation#ref497026

Chapter 4
Topological Semiotics of Visual Information

ABSTRACT

This chapter explains how active vision and image understanding can be implemented with topological semiotic models, using cognitive architecture with perceptual mechanisms similar to human vision.

INTRODUCTION

There were significant efforts in conversion image data into meaningful informational structures, and also on the usage of context in the processing of visual information. For instance, Geographic Information Systems (GIS) can adequately address problems with geographic and satellite imagery, because geographic knowledge has been well formalized in the form of maps, and maps can be represented well in digital form.

In the field of multimedia, the MPEG-7 standard was an extensive industry effort to address these problems for generic images, converting them into XML structures. MPEG-7 provides a set of image primitives called Descriptors. The MPEG-7 Description Scheme is the structure and semantics of the relationships between image components, which may be both Descriptors and Description Schemes. A MPEG-7 image description consists of a Description Scheme and a set of Descriptor Values.

MPEG-7 supports a range of abstraction levels, from low-level video features, such as are object's shape, size, texture, color, movement, and

DOI: 10.4018/978-1-5225-2431-1.ch004

position, to high-level semantic information. However, the MPEG-7 standard reflects the present state of image/video processing, and it only provides a set of predefined descriptors and schemas. MPEG-7 Visual Descriptors evolve from low-level image processing, which is well understood and formalized. However, Description Schemas relate to mid- and high-level image processing, which has not yet been well formalized.

Neither automatic and semi-automatic feature extraction nor schema creating algorithms is within the scope of the MPEG-7 standard. Although most low-level features can be extracted automatically, high-level features and schemas usually need human supervision and annotation. Only the description format in MPEG-7 is fixed and not the extraction and transformation methodologies. These are the areas that must be addressed.

The highest level of image description is the semantic one, and MPEG-7 standardizes information on these levels. But the problem of transforming primary image structures directly into semantic description has not been solved yet, as processes on the intermediary levels are not well understood and formalized.

Although RDF is better than other schemas in its ability to specify relationships and graphs, the MPEG-7 Group has made a decision to use an easily understandable and readable XML Schema Language as the MPEG-7 DDL. However, neither RDF nor XML Schema has been designed to describe complex dynamic hierarchical structures that constitute most of the real images.

MPEG-7 Visual Descriptors can be used for searching and filtering images and videos based on several visual features such as color, texture, object shape, object motion, and camera motion. This allows measuring the similarity between images and videos. Such a set of descriptors might be sufficient for the entire image.

Similar to MPEG-7 approaches convert images into their structured description that is based on low-level image features and their combinations, which use either top-down or bottom-up flow of processing image data or both types of flow, and attaching linguistic values for semantic querying. Most of them are trying to convert the image into a sort of structural description that can be compared against a similarly described collection of images stored in a database. (See Figure 1)

These approaches might work well for image and multimedia databases as they allow for creating structured collections of images, and querying them on certain similarity criteria, but not for the systems that must perform in the real-time and hostile environments. These approaches are not able to provide the needed level of understanding of the environment.

Figure 1. MPEG-7 and multimedia applications

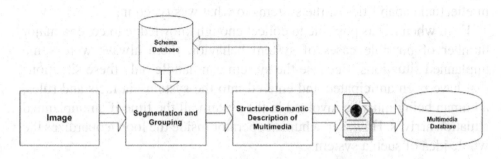

It is well known that expert systems (See Figure 2) in the late 80's and early 90's proved themselves to be ineffective in most areas of potential application. They were based on semantic principles, and processed data represented as language constructs. Semantic representation is good for knowledge acquisition from language, serving as a mediator between human experts and computers.

Figure 2. Expert systems: ontologies vs. a full-scale real-world knowledge system

Expert System <==> Ontologies

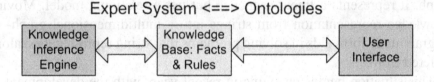

Full-Scale Real-World Knowledge System

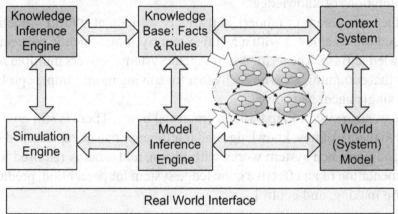

But it does not work well for modeling of intellectual processes. That limited intellectual capabilities of the systems to what was typed in.

Even when it was possible to collect enough knowledge to cover a major number of possible cases of system behavior, there always were some unplanned situations. Because the system can handle only these situations that have been anticipated and entered into the system via facts and rules, a human being must be involved in the system all the time if an unplanned situation arrives. However, a human operator inside the loop jeopardizes the whole idea of such a system.

If we look at the commonalities among all known knowledge models, we can find that knowledge has a hierarchical, relational nature, and knowledge models can be expressed in the form of graphs and diagrams. The first systems of writing were based on pictorial representation rather than on symbolic strings, and they look like pictorial diagrams that show the story in space and time.

Diagrams inspired scientists and philosophers such as Charles Sanders Pears to create abstract logical systems. After recognizing the failure of expert systems, there was an intensive search of more natural ways of representing knowledge, such as graph and diagrammatic models.

A string is a chain of symbols, whereas a chain is a flat and one-dimensional graph. It represents a linear sequence but not a relational model. Moving knowledge representation from strings into a multidimensional graph- or diagrammatic form aids in solving problems that string representation alone suffered from.

This situation begins changing in recent years with the development of multi-agent systems, methods of computational intelligence, and theories of visual languages, graph- and diagram-based representations and other natural representations of knowledge.

In the mainstream of modern software development, World Modeling is supposed to be achieved with a Multi-Agent System, which is connected to a Knowledge Base. The term "Multi-Agent Systems" covers multiple sets of agents that communicate with each other for solving more complex problems than a single agent can solve.

Today, such systems are built on empirical bases. There is still no widely accepted theory of how knowledge and intelligence can be represented in the brain and how such system works with vision, and what is required for the implementation of an effective knowledge system for perception, prediction, decision making, and control.

Any World Model can be described as a System. A System has an identifiable hierarchical, relational structure. However, it is impossible to have a complete set of models for every possible situation. Knowledge is incomplete in this sense. Instead, it helps to build models on the fly from smaller but verified models.

Knowledge Models include facts and rules. Facts are small fragmentary models of the World that are believed to be true. Rules are generalized models, where real entities are replaced with classes or roles. When such models come together in an active space, they tend to create a larger model.

However, traditional expert systems are based on symbolic strings of a written human language, and string representation of data cannot serve well to the purposes of creation a dynamic real-world knowledge system model that is a graph.

For that, we need such a knowledge representation that:

- Allows for the conversion of perceptual information into knowledge structures.
- Can provide a reliable description of contextual information.
- Allows for easy search or derivation/inference of new knowledge models and their incorporation into the knowledge base. Decision making is a subclass of such processes.

Network-symbolic models can match all the criteria above. Knowledge representation with Network-Symbolic models has a better modeling capability than the traditional ways of knowledge representation based on symbolic strings of written human language. In this case, the nature of the knowledge system rather than the appearance is a subject for modeling. The working unit here is a space. A relevant space is loaded into memory, which is equivalent to the activation of the space in the cortex while irrelevant spaces remain inactive.

A symbolic space represents a finite but modifiable set of implicit symbols ("alphabet"), which can denote features, objects, patterns, or any elements of the set. (See Figure 3) Methods of working with symbolic spaces can be based on learning and recognition (neural networks, etc.) or structural transformations (graph compression, etc.).

A model space captures relations between such "symbols" and allows for creation hierarchical network models (graphs, diagrams, plans, etc.) Network-Symbolic representation provides a natural basis for inference engines as the inference is a network transformation, which can be easily formalized.

Figure 3. Implicit symbols and their alphabets. This figure is illustrating methods of emerging implicit symbols and their alphabets in the brain that also can be achieved with methods of computational intelligence. There are no explicit symbols in the brain, but intelligent processes have symbolic nature. Informational representations of resonance are bell-shaped functions. Dynamics of a neural network can be represented as an energy landscape with local minima as attractors. The introduction of certainty dimension or normalization converts such a function into a fuzzy set. Fuzzy sets can be represented as implicit symbols in certainty dimension. The topological relations between such implicit symbols represent a graph or diagram-like structure, which is a basis of intelligent operations. Methods of computational intelligence that can create such implicit symbols are fuzzy sets, supervised and unsupervised neural networks, etc.

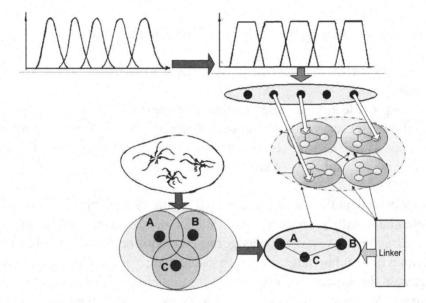

Genetic algorithms can optimize networks in search for better models. Logic is a way of packing these networks into consistent models.

A large number of methods and algorithms of low-level vision and image processing have been already accumulated in research, and such algorithms can be re-used via a set of interfaces. Network-Symbolic models provide a framework for binding of methods and algorithms for image processing, pattern recognition, and computational intelligence into a single system to choose optimal methods and algorithms.

Knowledge representation in the form of Network-Symbolic models allows for the emulation of low-, mid-, and high-level vision mechanisms on the same basis. Conversion of images into Network-Symbolic relational structures replaces the ill-posed problem of recognition with a solvable problem of understanding, where derivative relational structures are subject to comparison and not the primary views.

ECOLOGICAL MODEL OF VISUAL SCENE

Modern image analysis interprets an image as a 2-dimensional array of visual pixels by the laws of physical optics. This approach segments an image with further grouping into meaningful regions that represent surfaces and objects in the image. It has already become clear that this process must include top-down algorithms involving knowledge. However, this is not a trivial task, and it cannot be done without additional constraints. But where can these constraints come from?

Although fusion of visual data with data coming from active sensors can be very helpful in assigning relative distances to the elements of the visual scene, it might not always be a good choice for the combat situation. When the enemy equipped with a sort of "radar detector" devices that allow for the detection of scanning by an active sensor, this scanning can cause deadly counter-measures. Therefore, it would be better to rely more on passive sensors to remain unnoticed at least for the initial phase of the combat.

One of the biggest problems of modern image interpretation is that an image is treated as a 2-dimensional array of visual pixels in accordance with the laws of physical optics. Such a general approach requires the initial segmentation of an image with further grouping into meaningful regions that represent surfaces and objects in the picture. The outcomes can be used for further interpretation and recognition by humans or machines. It has already become clear that this process must include top-down algorithms involving knowledge. However, this is not a trivial task, and it cannot be done without additional constraints. But where can these constraints come from?

The visual system of vertebrates evolved to process visual information from the surrounding world efficiently. In his famous book on the ecological approach to visual perception, Gibson (2000) showed that the laws of physical optics could not explain the phenomenon of visual perception. He proposed a different approach that includes the ecological constraints.

According to Gibson (2000), the world always has fundamental properties, such as the ground plane where an animal stands. Vestibular organs of the animal disambiguate its position on the ground plane. The position and orientation of the animal's head and eyes are constrained by the anatomy of the animal. The sky usually is at the top part of the visual scene. The horizon is a visible line where the ground plane meets with the open air.

The distances from the animal to distant points or objects can be categorized into a few distinctive zones on the ground plane. There are no precise bounds between zones. However, both the ecological value of visual information and the ways of its processing differs in different zones.

A zone, which includes ranges to reachable surfaces and objects, can be described as a linguistic value "near." Objects in this zone can pose an immediate threat. The visual information here changes fast and requires fast processing and automatic reactive behaviors. Stereopsis is used for actions in this particular zone.

The most remote zone is closest to the horizon and can be described with the linguistic value "far." Visual information in that zone usually changes slowly. Objects in that zone usually do not pose an immediate threat, and visual information from that zone allows for longer analysis. Stereopsis does not play a significant role here.

There are perspective transformations in size of the same or similar visible objects that reside in different places on the ground plane between the observer's location and the horizon. Knowledge of those natural constraints helps effectively disambiguate visual information, adding an imaginary third dimension to the 2-dimensional image.

An image/video interpretation system must implement a set of ecological constraints, which predefine the ways of interpretation of information in its visual buffer. In this case, the lowest part of an image considered as a "near" zone of the ground plane. Part of the image from the bottom up to the horizon considered as a ground plane with the landscape. The zone in the middle of the image, which is closest to the horizon, shall be considered as relatively "far" from the observer. Relative distances between the points of the landscape shall be determined up from the very bottom until the horizon.

There are objects and surfaces on the ground plane. Visual sizes of similar objects reduce with increasing distances from the observer. Such transformations are called perspective and can be visualized with converging lines. The implicit lines can be represented by chains of elements in a discrete environment like visual buffer with receptive fields. The chains represent distances from the observer and in combination with network-symbolic structures like metric devices they can be used for sizes and proportion evaluations.

This ecological model of the visual scene is a network-symbolic structure, which has both discrete and continuous components. This is the initial set of constraints that can be applied for interpretation of receptive fields in the visual buffer by ecological optics. The idea of Ecological Model of Visual Scene is shown in Figure 4. Different types of environment can have different Ecological

Figure 4. Visual buffer and ecological optics. The ecological model is a set of ecological constraints that allows for interpreting the content of the visual buffer as a visual description of the 3-dimensional world. The world has some basic properties, such as the ground plane, where the observer stands. The position and orientation of the observer's head and eyes are constrained by the anatomy of vertebrates. The nearest to observer part of the ground plane is always under the observer's legs and is in the lowest part of the visual image. Therefore, the lowest part of a picture can be considered as a ground plane, which spreads from the observer up to the horizon line where it meets the sky. The part of the ground plane closest to the horizon is also farthest from the observer. Object sizes on the ground plane reduce with distances from the observer's location. Such transformations are called perspective and can be visualized with a convergent bundle of lines shown as white arrows on the image. Lines can be represented by chains of elements in a discrete environment like the visual buffer with receptive fields, and network-symbolic structures like metric devices can be used here for evaluation of sizes and proportions. An ecological model of the visual scene is a network-symbolic structure that allows for interpretation of the visual buffer in terms of ecological optics and for the assignment of relative distances and proportions.

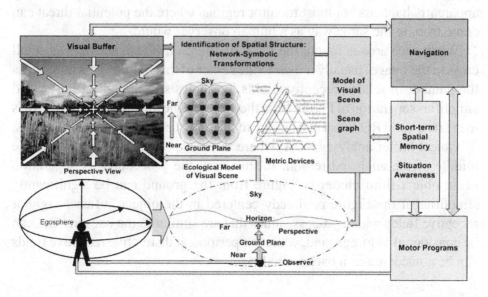

Models that provide different constraints and context for interpretation of the visual buffer. However, there are common ways of interpreting these network-symbolic structures as models of the 3-dimensional world.

The idea of Ecological Model of Visual Scene is shown in Figures 5 and 6. Different types of environment can have different Ecological Models that provide constraints and context for interpretation of the visual buffer. However, without having such a model, it is simply not possible to interpret a visual buffer. A human acquires such ecological visual knowledge shortly after birth. In the case of computer vision systems or target detection and identification systems, such knowledge should be incorporated into the system in a design phase.

An extraction of important objects from a visual scene is a serious problem in modern image analysis. Traditional bottom-up segmentation-grouping algorithms cannot handle this problem properly. Results are usually ambiguous and do not match the performance of a human. Top-down methods that do not consider ecological constraints also cannot help much. The problem of separation of an object from clutter is not just a problem of splitting a two-dimensional array by distinctive features.

The region of attention (ROA) is a part of the visual buffer, where receptive fields indicate the presence of distinctive, coherent features and the combinations that might constitute a particular object. In the simplest case, surrounding receptive fields do not show the presence of such features. However, in real situations, it is often hard to separate a target from a background. Therefore, the system should not only react to something apparently happens but must monitor regions where the potential threat can come from in the same way as a human observer would.

When such area is found, the focus of attention (FOA, shown as a small cross in the image) usually moves to the center of this region. This minimizes the number of related receptive fields for analysis in the object buffer and simplifies separation of Figure from the ground. The job of attention system is to create a valid ROA that can be sent to the object buffer for precise analysis.

Object buffer analyses ROA, where the focus of attention resides in the middle of the analyzed region. In this case, the procedures of separation of an object from clutter or Figure from the ground can be significantly simplified if the Figure is already centered in the object buffer. Neighbor receptive fields which possess values that are similar to the ones in FOA can be considered as foreground, while the peripheral distinctive receptive fields can be considered as a background.

Figure 5. Another example of visual buffer and ecological optics. An ecological model of the visual scene is a network-symbolic structure that allows for interpretation of the visual buffer regarding ecological optics and the assignment of relative distances and proportions (part of the images used herein were obtained from IMSI's MasterClips/ MasterPhotos Collection, 1985 Francisco Blvd. East, San Rafael, CA 94901-5506).

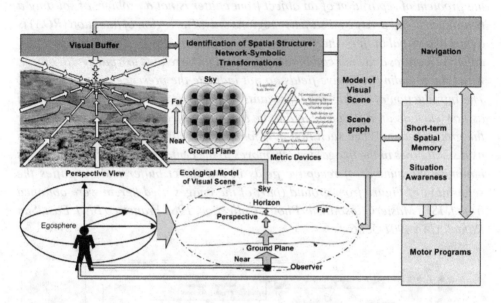

OBJECT PROCESSING IN THE FOVEAL OBJECT BUFFER

When visual information appears in the object buffer, it is important to restrict analyzed information to the area where the object resides, moving FOA to the center of the object. That means that the object buffer cannot be just a passive storage, but it must actively review and renew its content until it can stabilize FOA in the center of the analyzed object (see Figure 7).

A human being analyzed a moving object, in the same way, tracking the object and keeping the focus of attention in the center of the analyzed object (Coventry et al., 2010). In this case, changes in the object appearance become translations and rotations of the object components. The size of the region of attention might change. However, derivative structures such as skeletons are invariant to translation and rotation as they reflect topology or connectedness of the object and its components. This allows for the recognition of objects as exemplars of a class.

Hierarchical clustering of neighbor receptive fields is responsible for the understanding and classification of shapes and forms. A partition tree or a

Figure 6. Selection of an object from a visual to object buffer and the focus of attention. An extraction of important objects from a visual scene is a serious problem. Traditional bottom-up segmentation-grouping algorithms cannot handle this issue; results are always ambiguous and do match to the results obtained by a human. Top-down methods that do not consider ecological constraints also cannot help as the problem of separation of an object from clutter is not a problem of splitting a two-dimensional array by distinctive regions only. The region of attention (ROA) is a part of a visual buffer, where receptive fields indicate the presence of distinctive, coherent features and their combinations that might be related to a particular object, while the rounding receptive fields do not indicate the presence of such features. The introduction of ecological constraints helps set up a valid region of attention as now such an area is considered to be a distant object that resides on or above the ground plane. When such region is found, the focus of attention (FOA, shown as a small cross in the image) usually moves to the center of this region. This helps minimize the number of receptive fields in the object buffer and simplifies the separation of Figure from ground (part of the images used herein were obtained from IMSI's MasterClips/MasterPhotos Collection, 1985 Francisco Blvd. East, San Rafael, CA 94901-5506).

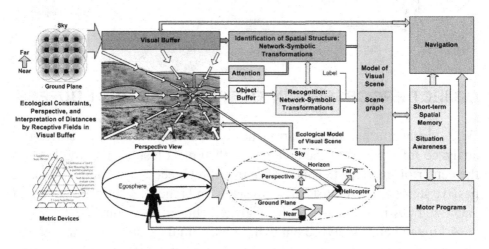

graph, which is built upon the hierarchically clustered receptive fields, can serve as a signature of a particular shape or form.

Derivative Structures are more abstract model structures that are created or derived from other model structures within the Network-Symbolic system. An example can be a skeleton graph or any other structure that identifies an object as exemplary of a class. Matching derivative structures rather than

Figure 7. Visual and object buffers

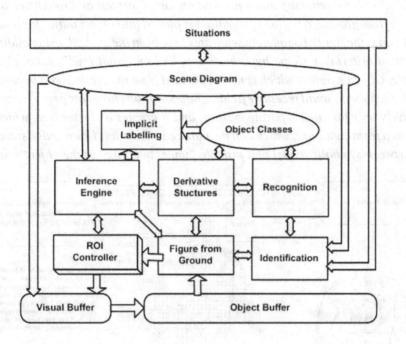

primary structures achieves the invariant classification of images. These processes are shown on Figures 8-9.

In the Network-Symbolic Models, not the original view but the derived structure is a subject for recognition. A skeleton graph can serve as an example of this derivative structure.

In past decades scientists debated if objects are recognized from sets of 2-dimensional views, or brain reconstructs 3-dimensional parametric models of the objects, which can be used for recognition. The computational approach treats the problem of 3-dimensional interpretation as a calculation of depth from disparities between matched features via equations of stereopsis. This problem can be solved if at least three views of an object and all other necessary constraints are known. However, it works perfectly only when we are in control of all the constraints of the image flow.

A 3-dimensional model of an object is a relational model of spatial order of its surfaces and their proportions. The spatial order can be represented as a connection graph. There is a generic logic of 3-dimensional structures, which is based on changes of relational structure in the visual or object buffer. This

Figure 8. Analysis of pattern or object in the object buffer of a network-symbolic system. After the narrowing down the first region of interest and rough separation of figure from ground, a region of attention is placed into object buffer for analysis. If necessary, the figure completely separates here from the ground, using additional separation criteria or shape hypothesis supplied by visual intelligence wherever possible. Object's figure, which is now separated from the ground, can be analyzed on a fine scale with small receptive fields. The bottom-up clustering process can work effectively only for such separate entities, and it creates a cluster tree, which can serve as a form signature, which can be analyzed by top-level knowledge structures as a network-symbolic model and provide "understanding" of the object's form.

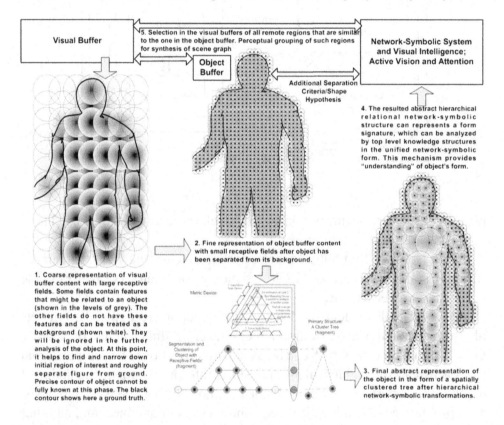

logic helps to build the connection graph. The proportions can be obtained with a structure like Size Measuring Device.

In the Network-Symbolic Models, not the original view but the derived structure is a subject for recognition (See Figures 10-11). Recognition becomes invariant to local changes and appearances of an object from a set of similar views. In this case, the number of needed views reduces to the ones that can

Figure 9. Process of analysis of pattern or object in the network-symbolic system (continued). The bottom-up clustering process can work effectively only for such separate entities, and it creates a cluster tree, which can serve as a form signature, which can be analyzed by top-level knowledge structures as a network-symbolic model and provide "understanding" of the object's form. In addition to that, all remote regions in the visual buffer, which are similar to the one that is currently in the object buffer, are selected and bound into a relational structure that can be further used for the creation of scene graph.

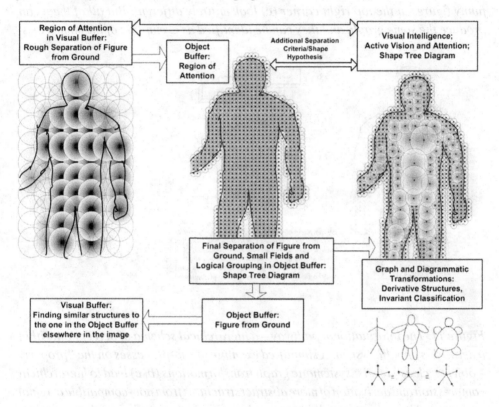

produce truly distinct structures. This creates an alphabet of possible views linked to the symbol of the object. Then object can be invariably recognized from different positions.

There is no way to transform primary image structure directly into the semantic description, skipping the intermediary levels. Separation of Figures from ground, derivation of structures, and multi-level decision making require a complex systematic environment. This cannot be done with a single method for real-world images. (See Figures 12-14)

Figure 10. Hierarchical clustering of neighbor receptive fields is responsible for understanding and classification of shapes and forms. A partition tree or a graph, which is built upon the hierarchically clustered receptive fields, can serve as a signature of a particular shape or form. Derivative Structures are more abstract model structures that are created, or derived from, other model structures within the network-symbolic system. An example can be a skeleton graph or any other structure that identifies an object as exemplary of a class. Matching derivative structures rather than primary structures achieves the invariant classification of images. Three funny figures at the top right corner (c) look entirely different. But all of them can produce the same graph, and they can be identified as exemplars of the same class.

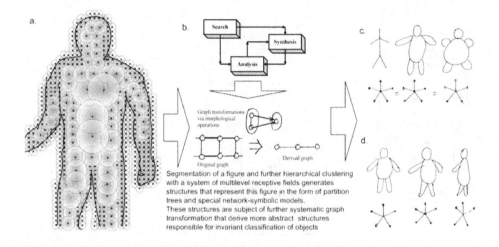

Figure 11. The informational pathway – a hierarchical schema of perception within a network-symbolic system. A simplified example of sub-processes on the "property – object – class" levels: systematic graph transformations (b, c) lead to hierarchical compression and derivation of more abstract structures from non-compatible original structures. That allows invariably recognize images as exemplars of the same class (d). Feedbacks provide context and resolve ambiguity and uncertainty.

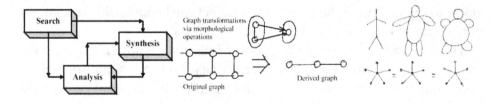

Figure 12. Holistic recognition and identification by parts as a single mechanism with closure links. In reality, this is a recursive process, because the same process also recognizes parts. Such mechanism saves response time wherever possible and provides a reliable recognition if the object is occluded, or complex, and cannot be recognized as a whole. Faces are recognized holistically, but recognition of texts always goes by parts. Complex objects must use both.

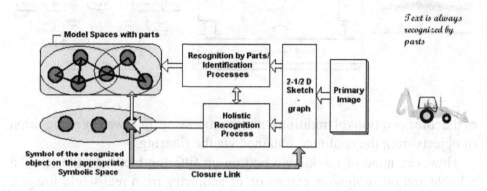

Figure 13. Visual surfaces as result of fusion of range features with spatial orientation features in the visual buffer

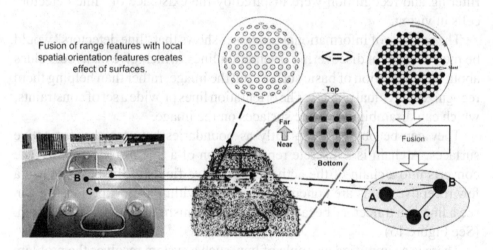

MAPPING SCENE GRAPH BACK TO VISUAL BUFFER

Perspective is one of the strongest visual cues, and orientation lines are global features that disambiguate the 3-dimensional environment presented on the image. Extraction of the edges and contours from images via filtering is one

Figure 14. A semantic description of an image can be done only on the highest level of Informational Pathway

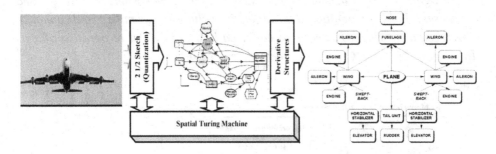

of the core operations of traditional image processing, followed by recognition of objects from the contours, obtained via the filtering.

However, none of the known bottom-up filtering methods allows for a reliable and unambiguous extraction of geometry from real-world images. Applying such filtering to real-world images usually transforms the image in most cases in such a way that it is not interpretable. This also negates all further efforts to extract any meaningful geometry from the image. Such filtering and recognition were inspired by the existence of "line detector" cells in vision.

The analysis of informational processes shows that "line detectors" would be more helpful in discovering orientation lines, which give observers clues about the orientation of basic surfaces on the image, rather than helping them recognize individual objects. The orientation lines provide a set of constraints, which can disambiguate basic surfaces on the image.

They can be obtained explicitly as boundaries between the distinctive surfaces. A chain is a discrete representation of a line or trajectory. A line converts into a chain of the activated receptive fields of the brain. When a few receptive fields are coherently activated within a short period, we can see a line or a trajectory because a brain mechanism links them into a chain. (See Figure 15)

There is a simplified example of how such a system resolves the problem of occluded contours. In the 2½-D sketch, a segment of line converts into a chain. Four visible segments converted to chains as the Model Spaces a, b, c, d. Such chain models can be easily linked into a larger chain.

Linker sets up links between Spaces a, b, c, d. It creates a larger Model Space A that represents an occluded contour. In simple cases, linking happens automatically, using simple criteria. But in more complex cases, it might

Figure 15. Graph representation of a line on the 2½-D sketch is a chain, where nodes denote the same feature/symbol. This Figure illustrates the idea of "understanding" occluded contours. Linking neighbor nodes into a larger chain, the linking process creates a model space A, representing an occluded contour. The vision system can accept such model as a part of the visual scene, and use it for a further image analysis. The model also can be rejected as an optical illusion. In this case, the model space A will be destroyed, and original components a, b, c, d becomes available to other models. This example can be easily generalized for more complex cases. It is easy to link here similar neighbor nodes/spaces into a larger structure. Linking and resulted structure must meet certain logical criteria, would it be a simple nearest neighborhood or a complex logic of visual scene. This way, both simple visual phenomena, like clustering and complex visual phenomena, like gestalts, can be naturally produced in such system.

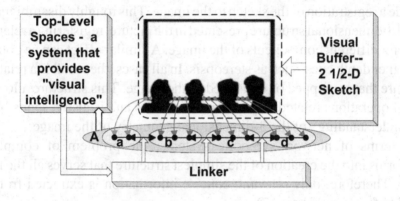

require a "visual intelligence" that only this environment can provide. The vision system verifies created models, using logics of the visual scene.

The visual system in its normal operation reduces objects to a sparse and compact representation. The significant advantage of the mechanism of Spaces is that it provides a "momentary learning," and handle spatial patterns repeated only in space, equally well as the patterns, repeated in time. Such situations are very common and known as the Gestalt laws. (Principles of grouping, 2017)

The lines in the middle of the image are chains of orientation features or symbols.

Gestalt laws describe how features are segmented and bound into perceived objects. Primary Gestalt principles are good continuation, closure, symmetry proximity, similarity, common motion, and co-linearity. These laws based on the spatiotemporal relationships between elements, and also predict a perception of Figure versus ground. Gestalt mechanisms are based on the binding and synchronization. The binding and synchrony are represented in our model as a graph. Clustering is a graph operation based on linking and binding of nearest neighbors and some metric criteria.

A visual scene has a certain logic, which allows using different cues for building network-symbolic relational structures from visual information. Similar features or symbols are clustered and linked together according to Gestalt laws (see Figure 16). Resulted orientation lines create a perspective that allows for assigning relational distances or depths on the sketch. Approximate distances are about the observer, and each other, and knowledge of some relative distances allow for deriving other relative distances.

The sketch is mapped back to the visual buffer via a set of closures, which provide a registration of the sketch to the image. This roughly disambiguates a global 3-dimensional structure presented in the picture, registering a relational depth for different components of the image. A similar effect can be obtained with other depth cues, such as stereopsis. In all cases, the result is a relational structure that is mapped or registered to the image. This structure allows for logical operations related to depth and distances and is also responsible for the "understanding" of the 3-dimensional geometry of the image.

In terms of network-symbolic systems, the problem of complexity transforms into the creation of the simplest structure that serves all the needs above. Therefore, only relevant, concise information is extracted from the visual buffer (See Figure 17).

In the real situations, like those depicted on Figure 17, the observer, an autonomous combat system equipped with target recognition, will have a very short time to react when it is ambushed by an enemy helicopter.

In the computer graphics, the mesh of primary objects and surfaces is computed from a scene graph. After mapping textures to mesh and applying lighting constraints, we receive a complete raster image.

In the case of image interpretation or understanding, the situation is the opposite. From an image, we need to obtain a scene graph, which is a top-level semantic description of an image. The visual information is ambiguous, and vision, in general, is not a linear process, but a combination of bottom-up and top-down processes. This is analogous to the puzzle, where some "islands of certainty," guesses about possible values and rules, help to complete it (See Figure 18).

Figure 16. An example of a mid-level vision process: perceptual grouping and analysis of gestalt with the system of active spaces. Primitive features are black and gray dots. Their symbols are a and b respectively (symbolic space 1). Model spaces 2 and 3 reflect the topology of black and gray columns respectively; model space 4 reflects the topology of a row. Further processes derive other model and symbolic spaces. Model spaces 2, and 3 create their symbols A on 5 and B on six, respectively, which denote black and gray columns. Their combination with 4 creates a more general description of gestalt on space 7. Generalization of primitive features with the abstraction of color creates a symbol of a generic dot on the symbolic space 8. Redundancy of links is necessary because it provides closures used for fast recognition. The process of derivation of spaces can continue while some regularity exists. For such system, symmetry is a just a topological feature. The same process will work for textures and other kinds of objects, providing a compact and self-describing code that will remain in the system even after the current content of the visual buffer is gone. Common parts of different images can be easily recognized. Activation of appropriate Space or Symbol by the Attention mechanism will activate relevant links and spaces and suppresses irrelevant ones. It leads to the separation of Figure from ground. Attention activation of symbol c on space seven will "separate" black columns from the image. Such process is natural in the system. It provides what S. Grossberg (1987) called "perceptual framing" – decomposition of the image by the set of components with "common fate"/common features, and their separate processing. Later, a combination of resulted graphs/spaces will produce a generalized graph of the entire picture that can be "understood." The processes of mid-level human vision work similarly.

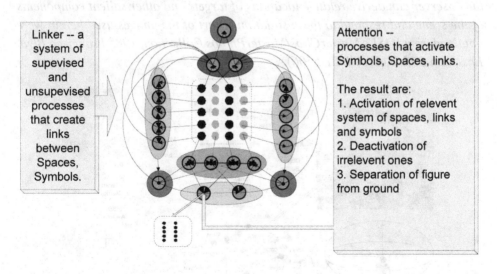

Linker -- a system of supevised and unsupevised processes that create links between Spaces, Symbols.

Attention -- processes that activate Symbols, Spaces, links.

The result are:
1. Activation of relevent system of spaces, links and symbols
2. Deactivation of irrelevent ones
3. Separation of figure from ground

Figure 17. The visual scene has a certain logic, which allows for using different cues in building network-symbolic relational structures from visual information. Once created, the scene graph changes slower than local information in the visual buffer. This allows for the mapping of labels and distances back to the visual buffer via a set of closures, which disambiguates visual information for action control and navigation (For the purpose of clarity, only one such closure for the helicopter object is explicitly shown on the current image. Such closures-links exist for other salient objects/regions, but the closures are not shown here. Semantic values are shown here only for a better explanation). Basic orientation lines extracted from the image are shown in black. White rectangles are samples of saccadic sequences, which examine details of a particular region and assign semantic values to the regions using their textures as features-symbols. The processes of identification of the spatial structure and recognition are interdependent. Recognition of texture as "bushes," or another type of vegetation, helps to "understand" surface as being of a particular type. Similarly, a surface can be treated as a "valley," and then the vegetation can be easier recognized as "bushes." An object, which suddenly popped up over the terrain, might not be recognized as a helicopter at the first moment. But its behavior and its position on the scene identify it as a helicopter, loading appropriate model and symbolic spaces for further recognition of the type of the helicopter and activation of appropriate reactive behavior. A similar logical mechanism works for spatial relations. Knowledge of some relative distances (solid arrows on the scene graph) make possible deriving other relative distances (dashed arrows on scene graph). Having the logic of visual scene captured in the form of relational, hierarchical network-symbolic structures and mapped back to the visual buffer, the observer can derive relative locations of targets and other salient components of the scene and respond to these situations (part of the images used herein were obtained from IMSI's MasterClips/MasterPhotos Collection, 1985 Francisco Blvd. East, San Rafael, CA 94901-5506).

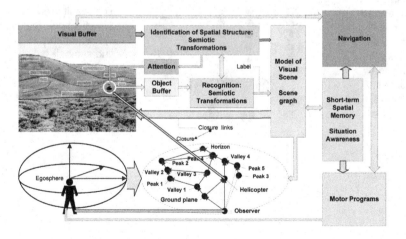

Figure 18. An image/video analysis that is based on network-symbolic principles differs from the linear bottom-up "segmentation-grouping-learning-recognition" algorithms of a traditional image analysis. Image/video understanding is not a single algorithm but a combination of recursive hierarchical bottom-up and top-down processes. It uses knowledge for disambiguation; and if we do not have any prior knowledge that can be matched to the image, then the image is simply not interpretable, just as an abstract painting might not be. The first phase creates a coarse global structure of the image. It is hard or, even impossible, to use geometric operations for natural image information. However, relational information is always available. When the brain builds a relational network-symbolic structure of a visual scene, it uses different clues to set up the relational order of surfaces and objects on the observer and each other. Feature, filter, symbol, and predicate are equivalent in network-symbolic systems. A linking mechanism binds these features/symbols into coherent structures, and in this way, image information converts from a "raster" into a "vector" representation. Orientation lines provide a set of constraints, which can disambiguate underlying surfaces on the image. In the case of textures, the direction of linking chains of neighbor textons is responsible for the effect of the texture gradient. A 3-D model of an object is a relational model of the spatial order of its surfaces and their proportions. The spatial order can be represented as a connection graph. There is a generic logic of 3-D structures, which is based on relational changes of object views in the visual or object buffers. This logic helps build the connection graph, while the proportions can be obtained from a special structure playing a role of a size measuring device.

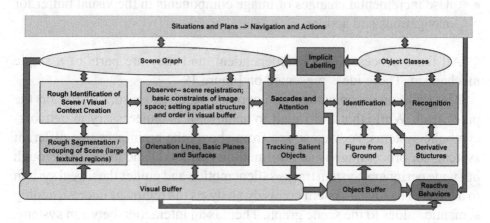

A view-based object recognition is a hard problem for traditional recognition algorithms that directly match a primary view of an object to a model. In Network-Symbolic Models, the derived structure and not the primary view is a subject for recognition. In this case, the number of possible object views reduced to those that can produce truly distinct structures. The resulting alphabet of such views is linked to the symbol of the object, and then the object can be invariably recognized from different positions. Such recognition is not affected by local changes and appearances of the object as seen from a set of similar views.

The problems with computer vision do not relate to imprecision or lack of particular methods. The solution of this problem requires an integrative framework that can:

- Mimic the spatial relational structure of salient information of an image in the form of an abstract hierarchical knowledge model instead of the precise reconstruction of a 3-dimensional model.
- Interpret or recognize important components of the image, implicitly labeling such relational structure.
- Map obtained relational structure back to the visual buffer via a set of closures for fast interpretation/understanding of visual information and use it for navigation and action tasks.
- Make decisions about actions and navigation.
- Use incremental changes of image components in the visual buffer for navigations and actions.

All these processes are interdependent, and they are parts of a single mechanism. These ideas presented on Figure 19.

The traditional computational approach requires sensors fusion on the pixel level. While this is difficult to achieve, it is unnecessary in network-symbolic systems. As we can see from above, the brain uses two different systems for processing visual information: peripheral and foveal. The rough but wide peripheral system tracks salient motion and guides the foveal system to a target. The foveal system precisely analyses the region of interest, adding semantic values to the scene graph. There is an interaction between systems that allows for creating "situation awareness."

Different sensor systems have differing capabilities. Some of them can better discriminate a target from clutter because of specific target features but do not have enough precision to identify what the target is. Others obtain better resolution of images but have to be pointed to the target location when the time is the at most importance. Thus, the situation is similar to the one that exists in the living creatures.

In the brain, fusion occurs as an interaction between the foveal and peripheral systems, and this interaction allows for building a scene graph from the visual buffer and situation awareness for the observer. The scene graph is a relational network-symbolic structure, which carries relational information about the salient objects/regions of the real world and can be mapped back to the visual buffer, making possible disambiguation of visual information and appropriate reactive behaviors. In such a statement of the problem, different sensors can refine the scene graph, and this requires a mechanism with associated reactive behavior, that points the various sensors in the particular region of interest. In humans, this mechanism is called "attention." In target recognition systems, this will require a controller driven by a top-down process from the scene graph that points all of the sensors in the same region of interest (see Figures 20-21).

Recognition allows the labeling of this structure with implicit symbols. Implicit labeling does not require explicit wording, and semantic values are shown here only for a better explanation. The processes of identification of the spatial structure and recognition are interdependent. Recognition of texture as the "grass" helps one "understanding" surface as a "meadow." From another side, the surface under vehicle wheels can be treated as a "meadow," and then the texture of surface can be easier recognized as "grass."

A similar logical mechanism also works for spatial relations. Approximate distances are about the observer, and each other, and knowledge of some relative distances (solid arrows on the scene graph) allow deriving other

Figure 19. The process of building and refining scene graph might require a temporary pointing different sensor subsystems to the region of interest chosen by the attention mechanism. It is easier to achieve fusion on this level rather than on the pixel level that is required by a traditional computational approach.

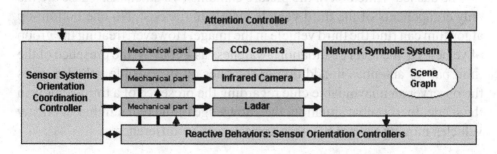

Figure 20. The solution to ATR problems cannot be given as a single method but rather requires a systematic framework, which combines bottom-up and top-down methods. A reliable holistic recognition of a target from a particular view might be only possible for a non-occluded, non-cluttered object, directly activating its implicit symbol on the appropriate symbolic spaces via a bottom-up process. Otherwise, the target can be identified only as a relational combination of its visible parts that activate appropriate model space linked to the symbol of the target. In fact, this is a recursive process, because individual parts can also be recognized or identified in the same way. Scene context and visual intelligence significantly increase the chances of identifying occluded targets.

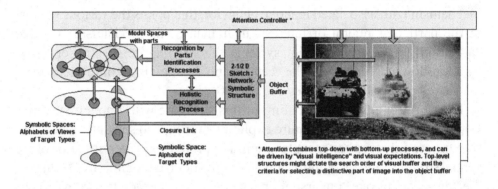

relative distances (dashed arrows on scene graph). The visual scene has certain logics, which allow using different cues for building network-symbolic relational structures from visual information.

Once built, the scene graph changes slower than the local information in the visual buffer. It allows the mapping of labels and distances back to the visual buffer via a set of closures, which disambiguates visual information for action control and navigation. This image also shows a possible use of "visual intelligence." A white rectangle in the picture means the content of object buffer obtained from saccade sequence.

The dashed white box in the picture contains two antennas. These are the only components of the third vehicle visible in the dust. No one bottom-up algorithm can find the third vehicle in the image. However, treating the group of vehicles at the level of situation awareness as a convoy, the presence of the third pair of antennas in addition to the ones on two visible vehicles gives the observer an unavoidable clue regarding the presence of a third vehicle in the scene. In a combat situation, the knowledge of the real number of enemy vehicles moving toward the observer can make a difference.

Figure 21. An example of analysis of the visual buffer and situation awareness with a system of active vision based on the network-symbolic models. Instead of precise calculations of a 3-dimensional model of the visual scene, the brain reconstructs a spatial relational structure of salient information from the visual buffer using different depth cues on the observer placed in the center of "Egosphere."

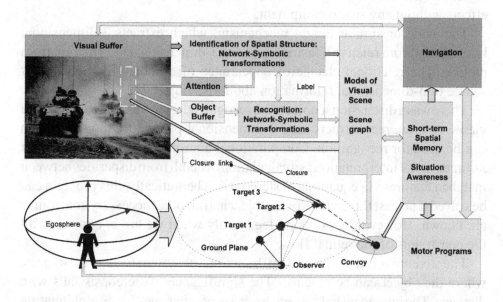

The foveal system can be considered acuity window. This window is moving within the visual buffer to build a spatial map. The spatial map feedbacks to the visual buffer via closures, and this is equivalent to image labeling and depth marking. The saliency of visual information is depicted on the spatial map, which also is a scene graph.

Foveal vision processes the salient components of the image. When we focus attention on an object, it usually looks clear and precise, while the background is slightly blurred. The foveal system treats the object as a Figure, while the peripheral vision gives a broader picture of the entire scene, and helps in motion control.

The research found cells in the primate visual cortex that react to movement in a particular direction. Motion in a particular direction can be considered a vector. This means that we might have alphabets of symbols that represent vectors, as we have alphabets of static features. This allows an unambiguously separate object, which is moving relatively to its background, and observe kinetic boundaries as clear object boundaries that might otherwise be blurred.

121

An object tracking system keeps the analyzed object in the center of the fovea. A tracking mechanism reduces object motion to scaling and rotation. The former can be used for disambiguating spatial order of visual scene, while the latter reveals the 3-dimensional structure of an object. In high-quality color movies, rotating objects sometimes display stunning 3-dimensional effects without any stereo equipment.

The same or similar neural mechanism, which extracts 3-dimensional information from relative disparity, extracts 3-dimensional information from motion. The relational change of appearance of an object is the primary source of 3-dimensional information about this object.

There was a discussion if objects are recognized from sets of 2-dimensional views, or brain reconstructs their 3-dimensional parametric models, which can be used for recognition. Computational approach treats the problem of 3-dimensional interpretation as a calculation of depth from disparities between matched features via equations of stereopsis. Theoretically, this problem can be solved if at least three views of an object and all other necessary constraints are known. However, it works perfectly only when we are in control of all the constraints of the retinal flow.

The stereopsis is heavily used by the action subsystem for short distances, where the object can be reached. The significance of stereopsis falls with distance. The human visual system uses a set of other cues for disambiguating 3-dimensional information at different distances from the observer.

We do not know precisely the depth or distance to a particular point. But we usually know that the object A is closer to us than a surface B. When moving or acting, we also do not make precise calculations. But we usually know how long it will take for us to get there if we move with a particular speed, or how an object should be reached and grasped.

Our motion routines use incremental relational changes of information in the visual buffer instead of precise numeric calculations. Such relational changes have a certain logic, which can be used for navigation and actions. An example of a qualitative description of such a routine on the top level is: "Navigate toward object A (a landmark) while its size increases until you can reach it; turn left; move toward surface B."

In other words, the brain uses the relational principle to set up the spatial order of information in the visual buffer.

A 3-dimensional model of an object is a relational model of spatial order of its surfaces and their proportions. The spatial order can be represented as a connection graph. There is a logic of 3-dimensional structures, which is based on changes of relational structure in the visual or object buffer. This logic helps to build the connection graph. The proportions can be obtained with a structure like Size Measuring Device.

The brain uses knowledge of object for actions, and action models are usually connected with navigation. But the problem of navigation in the 3-dimensional environment requires a view-based approach. A ground observer must identify primary surfaces on the scene, their orientation, and spatial order relatively to other surfaces and the observer. Horizontal surfaces can be directly used for navigation, while vertical surfaces just constrain available space. Differently oriented surfaces reflect light differently, and they are presented in the retinal image as distinct regions.

It is hard, or even impossible, to use geometric operations against natural image information. However, relational information is always available. When the brain builds a relational network-symbolic structure of the visual scene, it uses different clues to set up the relational order of surfaces and objects on the observer and each other.

In computer graphics, the mesh of primary objects and surfaces is computed from a scene graph. After mapping textures to mesh and applying lighting constraints, we receive a complete raster image.

In the case of image interpretation or understanding, the situation is the opposite. From an image, we need to obtain a scene graph, which is a top-level semantic description of an image. The visual information is ambiguous, and vision, in general, is not a linear process, but a combination of bottom-up and top-down processes. This is analogous to the puzzle, where some "islands of certainty," guesses about possible values and rules, help to complete the puzzle.

To start the top-down processes, we need the initial top-level structure. It can be refined later or rebuild. Therefore, the first phase of our image analysis would be creating a coarse global structure of the image. Once it has been built, the top-level abstract network-symbolic model of scene changes slower than low-level details in the visual buffer. Therefore, the top-down process can disambiguate the mapping of lower-level features and objects, which change in the flow rapidly. This top-level model can be used for efficient spatial navigation and gaze control. In terms of network-symbolic systems, the problem of complexity transforms into the creation of the simplest structure that serves all the needs above. Therefore, only useful information should be extracted from the visual buffer.

The orientation lines provide a set of constraints, which can disambiguate basic surfaces on the image. They can be obtained explicitly as boundaries between the distinctive surfaces. A line converts into a chain of the activated receptive fields of the brain. When a few receptive fields, cortical columns, or even hypercolumns, are coherently activated within a short period, we can see a line, or a trajectory, because a brain mechanism links them into a chain. The chain is a structure, which gives us "understanding" of lines and trajectories.

The Linker mechanism binds features into coherent structures. A regular or a quasi-regular texture produces a grid structure if the symbols of textons are linked together. The orientation of linking chains gives the same impression as we can get from the orientation lines. This structure is responsible for the effect of the texture gradient.

Another clue comes from shading. A Normal line to a shaded surface gives a clue about local surface orientation. It can be obtained from a local filter. The filter, feature, symbol, and predicate are equivalent in the network-symbolic systems. If we link symbolic information into coherent structures, then we have a mesh or a sketch. This way, image raster-converts into a vector representation. This mesh or sketch is a relational model of a surface, and it also can be used for the "understanding" of relief or local surface.

Figures 22-25 demonstrate analysis of visual buffer and creation of a situation model with a system of active vision based on the network-symbolic models in different situations. Every visual scene always has certain logics, which allow using appropriate cues for building network-symbolic relational structures from the visual information. Recognition allows the labeling this structure with implicit symbols. Implicit labeling does not require explicit wording, and semantic values are shown there only for a better explanation.

Once built, the scene graph changes slower than the local information in the visual buffer. It allows the mapping of labels and distances back to the visual buffer via a set of closures. This disambiguates visual information for planning of motor activities and control of actions. Approximate distances are about the observer and each other, and knowledge of some relative distances allow deriving other relative distances on the scene graph.

Figure 23 demonstrates understanding of geometry and orientation of surfaces in the real world image. The sketch in the middle of Figure 23 cannot be obtained with any of the traditional bottom-up filtering methods. Extraction of the edges and contours from images via filtering is one of the core operations of traditional image processing, followed by the recognition of objects from the obtained contours.

None of the known bottom-up filtering methods allows for a reliable and unambiguous extraction of geometry from real-world images. This filtering

Figure 22. An example of reconstructing a spatial relational structure of salient information from the visual buffer using different depth cues on the observer placed in the center of "Egosphere." It is very hard to recognize individual bottles in the left part of the image by any bottom-up recognition algorithm. However, a top-down process of image understanding can logically identify this part of the image as a group of bottles, and this makes recognition of individual bottles in the group easy. A similar logical mechanism also works for spatial relations (part of the images used herein were obtained from IMSI's MasterClips/MasterPhotos Collection, 1985 Francisco Blvd. East, San Rafael, CA 94901-5506).

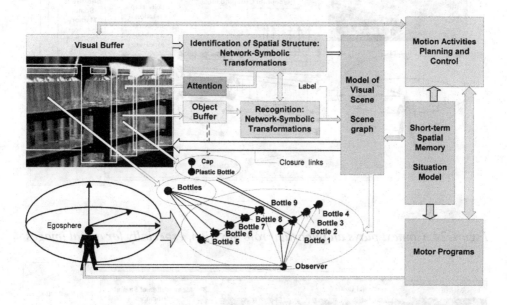

usually transforms an image in such a way that it is not interpretable, and it negates all further efforts to extract any meaningful geometry.

Such filtering and recognition were inspired by the existence of "line detector" cells in vision. However, the analysis of informational processes shows that "line detectors" would be more helpful in discovering orientation lines, which give observers clues about the orientation of basic surfaces on the image, rather than helping them recognize individual objects.

Approximate distances are relative to the observer and each other, and knowledge of some relative distances allows for deriving other relative distances. A similar effect can be obtained with other depth cues, such as stereopsis. The resulted relational structure is mapped or registered to the image.

Figure 23. An example of understanding real world geometry and orientation of surfaces (part of the images used herein were obtained from IMSI's MasterClips/ MasterPhotos Collection, 1985 Francisco Blvd. East, San Rafael, CA 94901-5506)

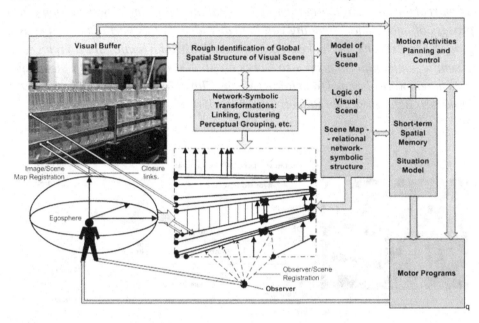

Figure 24. Context plays an important role in vision, especially for aerial images

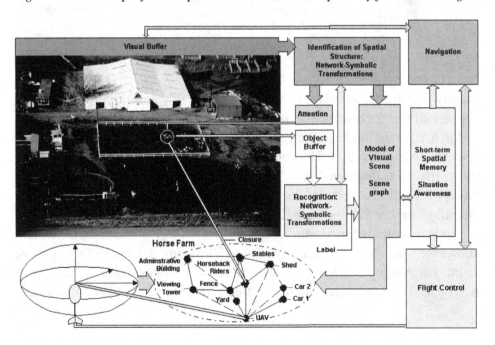

Figure 25. Recognition of texture as "asphalt," or another type of road cover, helps to "understand" surface like a road. From another side, the surface under car wheels can be treated as a "road," and then the road surface can be easier recognized as "asphalt." A similar logical mechanism also works for spatial relations (part of the images used herein were obtained from IMSI's MasterClips/MasterPhotos Collection, 1985 Francisco Blvd. East, San Rafael, CA 94901-5506).

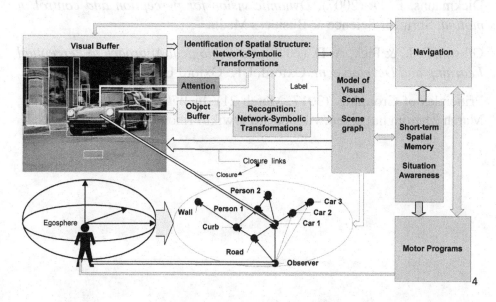

This structure is responsible for the "understanding" of the 3-dimensional geometry of the image.

Context plays an important role in vision, especially for aerial images. (See Figure 24) Context simply activates appropriate symbolic and model spaces that might be relevant to the situation. It is difficult to recognize small objects in the image as the horseback riders, not knowing the context. But identification of the context of an aerial image of a "horse farm" makes it easier to recognize those small objects as the horseback riders. Conversely, recognition of the horseback riders may aid in the identification of the context of an aerial image of a "horse farm." A similar logical mechanism also works for spatial relations. Mapping of labels and distances back to the visual buffer via a set of closures disambiguate visual information for action control and navigation.

REFERENCES

Coventry, K. R., Lynott, D., Cangelosi, A., Monrouxe, L., Joyce, D., & Richardson, D. C. (2010). Spatial language, visual attention, and perceptual simulation. Brain and Language, 112(3), 202-213.

Dickmanns, E. D. (2007). *Dynamic vision for perception and control of motion*. Springer Science & Business Media.

Gibson, E. J., & Pick, A. D. (2000). *An Ecological Approach to Perceptual Learning and Development*. Oxford, UK: Oxford University Press.

Principles of Grouping. (2017, March 21). In *Wikipedia*. Retrieved 2017, March 21 from https://en.wikipedia.org/wiki/Principles_of_grouping

Chapter 5
Practical Implementation Considerations

ABSTRACT

This chapter briefly describes APIs that could be used today for prototyping or implementing proposed architecture and methods.

INTRODUCTION

Functional active vision systems aren't new, and they been developed within the past decade. But they are based on the combo of traditional computational methods, and heavily rely on GPS. Such systems still may guarantee adequate safety neither for the human nor for themselves.

Autonomous vehicles and robots need much smarter perceptual and cognitive systems that will allow them remain one hundred percent safe for human and at the same time successfully accomplish more complex missions.

A distributed software environment that works with network-symbolic methods and models can be considered as a new flavor of multi-agent systems, and we can call a practical software realization as "Image/Video Understanding Engines" (by analogy with the "Speech Recognition Engines" -- software components used in the speech recognition software.)

The Engine needs to handle with Model and Symbolic spaces, and this requires special APIs. Model spaces API should be able to work with graphs; symbolic spaces API should be able to recognize patterns, create new implicit symbols, and provide hierarchical compression of the obtained results.

DOI: 10.4018/978-1-5225-2431-1.ch005

Relevant Spaces should be loaded from the underlying repository, linked, processed, and meaningful outcomes should be stored back to the repository. The system should be able to provide mechanisms similar to the activation of relevant Spaces and attention, as well as needed transformations via search, synthesis, and analysis cycle.

Besides that, the platform should have some low-level processing services, which comprise of visual and object buffers described above, and also buffer which does an active fusion of different visual features in the manner of 2-½ Sketch. And the system needs to plan and predict its behavior upon the generated situation awareness, which would be equivalent to the motor programs in the human cortex.

All these ideas are presented in Figure 1. The engine should be installed on an active vision platform, which is mandatory for autonomous systems, where Action, Perception, and Cognition should work in a coherent manner, which is shown in Figure 2 that depicts processes in the system. To describe those processes, we will be using terminology that is similar to human vision, although its technological implementation might be completely different.

The model of the visual scene is obtained via saccades and fixations. Visual information appears in the system as a retinal flow. Retinal flow

Figure 1. Image/video understanding engine

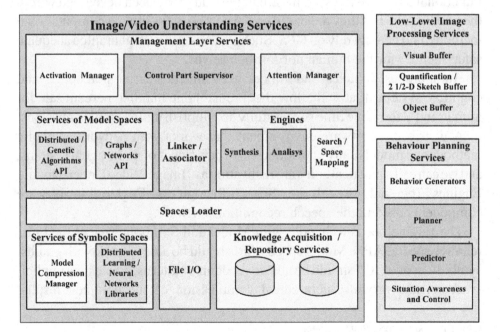

Figure 2. A system of active vision with network-symbolic models

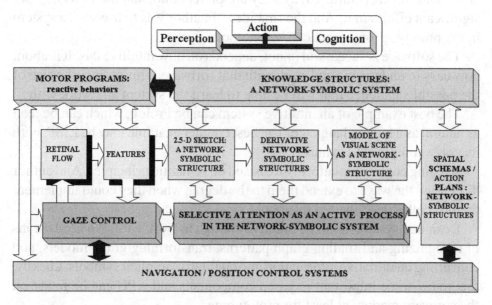

transforms into features or symbols, which are combined into a primary relational network-symbolic structure: 2.5D Sketch. This allows derivation of other network-symbolic structures like objects, switching attention to different sub-structures, processing them one at a time, and building a more abstract hierarchical model of the visual scene, which is accountable for image understanding and situation awareness of the observer.

The schema can be represented as a scene graph. In the real world situations, the top-level abstract network-symbolic model of the scene disambiguates lower-level features and objects, which change in the flow. Feedback projections help create unambiguous network-symbolic structures of the visual scene and map the obtained "symbols" (understanding) back to the primary image structure for navigation and action tasks. All processes in the system are interdependent. Incremental changes in the visual scene drive motion in the environment. Motion creates changes and disambiguates visual information.

When there is a need in a new software system, the first step is to look for the commercially available software that may either serve as a prototype, or proved some APIs and/or components. It may help to avoid reinventing the wheel.

There were multiple efforts to create cognitive platforms that can carry models of the World. Author could name a few of them such as CYC (CYC,

2017) and SOAR (Laird, 2012), they are pretty solid, and their creators put significant efforts in it. And the first idea of author was to use such a system in the prototype for a practical Autonomous System.

The software is successful or not, depends on how intuitive it is. It is about how easy to understand and work with that software. This defines the size of the possible audience that will be able to learn the system and work with it.

The best example of an intuitive system can be Prolog, which can be read as natural as a human language. The best counter example may be LISP, with its crazy complicated syntax.

Existing cognitive platforms are based on semantic principles. And author didn't find the ways to extend them to the degree when they could implement the principles described in this book.

Designed system has to be intuitive enough to work with. We need means of recognizing and finding graph patterns, transforming graph models, and converting quantitative information into qualitative implicit symbols. Luckily, that today some important required components and APIs can be found on the software market, at least for prototyping.

GRAPH DATABASES

The first thing that may be needed is some graph or diagrammatic repository.

In past decades there were multiple efforts to provide some efficient graph data storage. But they lacked an underlying physical mechanism that would allow for efficient manipulation of such data.

Due to their mainstream in usage, Relational Databases became dominating 99% of the market, and SQL was intensively studied in the universities as the only alternative. That led to the situation when Relational Databases were applied to the projects, which in reality would rather require drastically different kind of data storage.

A major problem with the relational database that it has all entities and relations hard coded and built into the schema, which is determined in the design phase. This approach is perfect for a General Ledger. But a small change to the relational database schema is usually extremely painful for the application that is working on top of this database.

By that reason, Relational Database may not be a good candidate for the graph storage.

NoSQL databases are a rapidly emerging segment of the software market. There are a few flavors of NoSQL databases:

- Key-Value Data Stores
- Document Data Stores
- Columnar Data Stores

None of them can serve the purpose of efficiently storing and manipulating graph data.

Luckily, there is the fourth flavor of NoSQL databases that directly serve this purpose – graph databases (Robison, Webber, and Eifrem, 2015), which recently started gaining a sufficient popularity.

Relationships are necessary components of the flexible graph data model. In other types of databases, connections between entities are inferred with foreign keys or map-reduce custom algorithms.

By assembling the abstractions of nodes and relationships into connected structures, graph databases allow building pretty sophisticated graph models.

A graph database management system is an online database management system with Create, Read, Update, and Delete (CRUD) methods that expose a graph data model. Graph databases are generally optimized for transactional performance, and engineered with transactional integrity and operational availability in mind.

Graph databases comprise of the underlying storage and processing engine. (See Figure 3)

Figure 3. Graph database structure (by Neo4j)

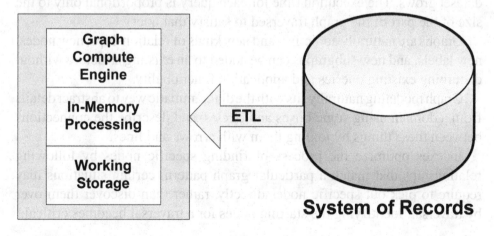

Graph databases storage is designed for graphs. Not all graph databases use native graph storage. Some may serialize the graph data into a relational database, an object-oriented database, or another data store.

Any database that exposes a graph data model through CRUD operations qualifies as a graph database. However, index-free adjacency provides the significant performance advantages for native graph processing.

Native graph storage is engineered for performance and scalability. Native graph processing requires that a graph database use index-free adjacency, meaning that connected nodes physically "point" to each other in the database. It benefits traversal performance. But some queries that don't use traversals are complicated or memory intensive.

Graph compute engine enables global graph computational algorithms to be run against large data sets. Because of their emphasis on global queries, graph computes engines are usually optimized for scanning and processing large amounts of information in batches, and in that respect, they are similar to other batch analysis technologies, such as data mining and OLAP.

A variety of different types of graph computes engines exist. A graph database provides a powerful data modeling technique with a sufficient justification for replacing relational data platform. On top of this performance benefit, graph databases offer an extremely flexible data model, and a mode of delivery aligned with today's agile software delivery practices.

A graph database has better performance than relational databases and NOSQL stores performance when dealing with connected data. In the relational databases join-intensive query performance deteriorates as the dataset gets bigger.

A graph database performance remains relatively constant, even as the dataset grows. The execution time for each query is proportional only to the size of the part of the graph traversed to satisfy that query.

Graphs are naturally addictive, and new kinds of relationships, new nodes, new labels, and new subgraphs can be added to an existing structure without disturbing existing queries and application functionality.

Graph modeling naturally fits with the diagrammatic way to abstract details from a domain using some boxes and circles, and describe the connections between these things by joining them with arrows and lines.

Indexes optimize the process of finding specific nodes by following relationships that match a particular graph pattern, certain situations may require to pick out specific nodes directly, rather than discover them over by traversal. Identifying the starting nodes for a traversal becomes critical.

A database engine that utilizes index-free adjacency is where each node maintains direct references to its adjacent nodes. This means that query is independent of the total size of the graph, and is proportional to the amount of the graph search.

Although graph databases are the natural candidates for using with the cognitive architectures and engines, there are some obstacles to overcome.

COGNITIVE APIS

Cognitive APIs are necessary to convert input data into the network-symbolic format. Due to the data analytics needs, some data analytics packages like Spark provide the capability for presenting input information in the Graph format for further analysis.

A serious problem is how to build a repository of cognitive semiotic models that will reflect real world knowledge. A major issue here is that most of the knowledge is encapsulated in the form of natural language texts, which should be turned into semiotic models.

Otherwise, the cognitive context will be lost. Also, communication with the autonomous system will be problematic. As it was said earlier, the solution of human tasks requires at least human level of intelligence. No animals had displayed a capability for that.

There are many NLP packages on the market. Major commercial companies provided their NLP implementations: IBM, Microsoft, Google, and Oracle. There are multiple others companies, which specializes in the NLP software. NLP is now a necessary component of data analytics, and NLP packages are also can be found in the Open Source, like for instance Python.

Those packages are supposed to discover a set of basic concepts and build vocabulary. They are also providing syntactical parsing and text annotations. However, this doesn't go much further. Obtained results are used either for statistical analysis or for creating some semantic network, which can serve the needs of specialized applications.

What is required: the semantic network is a private case of a semiotic model, where all nodes are hard coded explicitly. This should be changed slightly into the semiotic network-symbolic format, where all symbols are nodes of the network, they are linked to their linguistic labels, and they are forming alphabets based on their similarity and category. Verbs identify relations between such symbols. Extracted information is split by Model Spaces that describe the world facts or assertions, linking derived concepts.

Once we can create such models out of the texts, we could quickly fill the cognitive repository with world models that can be further used in the cognitive processes. These ideas are briefly depicted on Figure 4.

Multiple packages and services can be used in the design and development of cognitive semiotic systems. Author may suggest a few for prototyping that are currently available on the market, although this list is changing very rapidly.

IBM Watson Developer Cloud (2017) provides REST APIs and SDKs that use cognitive computing to solve complex problems. Cognitive services are adaptable, interactive, and contextual in the way they provide information.

Figure 4. Converting text into cognitive semiotic models: a) overall process; b) transformation of syntactic models stream into cognitive semiotic models

A. Building semiotic models from texts.

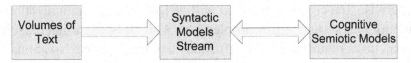

B. Converting syntactically parsed texts into semiotic models

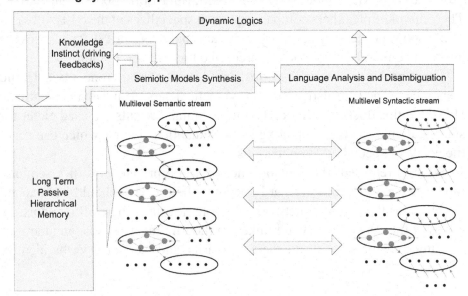

The IBM Watson Dialog Service allows a developer to design the way an application interacts with an end user through a conversational interface.

IBM Alchemy API offers three services that enable developers to build cognitive applications that understand the content and context of text and images.

IBM Alchemy Language is a collection of text analysis functions that derive semantic information from the input text, HTML, or a public URL and leverage sophisticated natural language processing techniques to get a quick, high-level understanding of the content and obtain detailed insights such as directional sentiment from entity to object.

It identifies concepts with which the input text is associated, based on other concepts and objects that are present in that text. Concept-related API functions understand how concepts relate and can identify concepts that are not directly referenced in the text. Concept Tagging enables higher level analysis of input content than just primitive keyword identification.

Entity extraction adds semantic knowledge to content to help understand the subject and context of the text that is being analyzed. The entity extraction techniques used by the Alchemy Language service are based on sophisticated statistical algorithms and natural language processing technology. It can specify a custom model in a request to identify a custom set of entity types in the content, enabling domain-specific entity extraction.

It identifies the subject, action, and object relations within sentences in the input content. After parsing sentences into subject, action, and object form, the Relation Extraction API functions can use this information for subsequent processing by other Alchemy Language functions.

Typed Relations uses custom models to recognize entities in content, and identifies various types of relationships between those entities. The types of entities and relations that can be identified are properties of the custom model that is specified.

Taxonomy categories input text, HTML or web-based content into a hierarchical taxonomy up to five levels deep.

Alchemy Language offers a wide variety of text analysis capabilities, but getting a wealth of semantic information for a single document is made simple with combined calls.

IBM Concept Expansion analyzes text and learns similar terms (words or phrases) based on context. It helps users to rapidly create a lexicon (a set of related terms) from a dataset of text fragments.

The IBM Natural Language Classifier service applies cognitive computing techniques to return the best matching classes for a sentence or phrase.

The IBM Visual Recognition service enables the user to analyze the visual appearance of images or video frames to understand what is happening in a scene.

IBM Watson service provided by Cognitive Scale, Cognitive Graphs are an encapsulation of knowledge, sourced from a 3rd party, internal, and private data sources, using domain specific models, into a query-able graph representation.

IBM also provides rich multiple machine learning APIs.

Microsoft provides Computer Vision API and Computational Network Toolkit API. They also provide various other APIs, but author's goal is to list here those that might be directly relevant to the subject of this book (Computer Vision API, 2017).

Google and Oracle also have their versions of similar APIs.

There is no need to have all available APIs listed in this book. A major reason is that it will become obsolete even before the book will be published.

Much more important is to understand what APIs can be needed for the purposes described in the book. Then it will become just a homework for the readers, who might be interested in the prototyping or development of cognitive semiotic systems to find the best APIs, which will be available at the time when they start such a prototyping or development.

REFERENCES

Computer Vision API. (2017). Microsoft. Retrieved from https://www. microsoft.com/cognitive-services/en-us/computer-vision-api

CYC. (2017, April 4). In *Wikipedia*. Retrieved 2017, April 04 from https:// en.wikipedia.org/wiki/CYC

Laird, J. E. (2012). *The SOAR Cognitive Architecture*. MIT Press.

Robinson, I., Webber, J., & Eifrem, E. (2015). Graph databases: new opportunities for connected data. O'Reilly Media, Inc.

Watson Developer Cloud. (2017). IBM. Retrieved from https://www.ibm. com/watson/developercloud/

Conclusion

The nature of perception does not allow separating it from the cognition. And without effective cognitive models, it is impossible to build effective practical machine perception systems.

Most of existing cognitive architectures are based on semantic/linguistic approaches, which have serious shortcomings. But cognition is not limited by language and logic only. The purpose of this book was to address existing disconnect between the mainstream of machine perception, based on bottom-up mathematical models of features, and new results of applied cognitive science.

Knowledge and order exist in topological semiotic structures, which may effectively describe systems, and logic appears to be a way of synthesis of such structures. That allows for creating multilevel conceptual models, which provide context for driving perception top-down and deep understanding of perceived information by autonomous systems for fast and efficient decision making.

Systematic approach allows representing such models in a graph or diagrammatic form that can be formalized and programmed. The semiotic approach allows for the universal representation of such graphs and diagrams.

Semiotics doesn't require explicit labeling of nodes, which was a major shortcoming for semantic models. A symbol here denotes a pattern on the upper level of hierarchy. And new symbols that label a node can be created on fly as result of recognition of a known pattern, or dynamic creation of a new pattern by a cognitive process.

That opens unlimited capability to work with structural systematic data, which reflect the order in world. Intelligent operations that always were a mystery simply turn into the operations on graphs, which could be well formalized and programmed.

This may effectively work for the accumulation of experience by autonomous systems. This book reviews basic mechanisms of perception, cognition, language, and their interaction in terms of the topological semiotic models framework, which can be supported by the evidence from neuroscience.

Interactions of processes in such hierarchical semiotic representation are essential for modeling cognition and perception, and creation efficient cognitive architectures necessary for making robots and unmanned vehicles really perceive and understand the world the way that humans do.

Many interesting points remained beyond the scope of this book due to its limited size: how implicit symbols can be built with neural networks, fuzzy sets, and dynamic fuzzy logic; how topological semiotic knowledge can be used for system context; how facts, rules, theories, classes, and hierarchies can be expressed in semiotics; how associations between concepts and other models create systems; how system dynamics can be extracted from texts; how plans and scenarios can be created from system models, etc.

However, the purpose of this book is not so much to provide a complete set of answers to all possible practical problems that have to be solved for making autonomous systems able perceiving and understand the world in the way that humans do. The purpose of this book is to give food for thought to the startup workers, industry practitioners, and computer and cognitive scientists to make this happen today.

Appendix

Figure 1.
Past

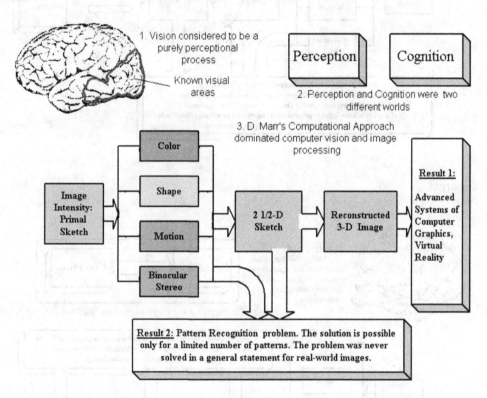

1. Vision considered to be a purely perceptional process

Known visual areas

Perception   Cognition

2. Perception and Cognition were two different worlds

3. D. Marr's Computational Approach dominated computer vision and image processing

Color

Shape

Image Intensity: Primal Sketch

Motion

2 1/2-D Sketch

Reconstructed 3-D Image

Binocular Stereo

Result 1:

Advanced Systems of Computer Graphics, Virtual Reality

Result 2: Pattern Recognition problem. The solution is possible only for a limited number of patterns. The problem was never solved in a general statement for real-world images.

Figure 2.
Current

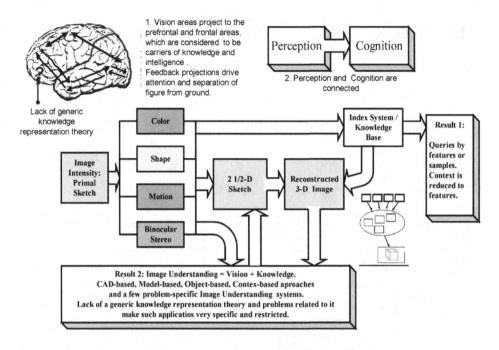

Figure 3.
Next

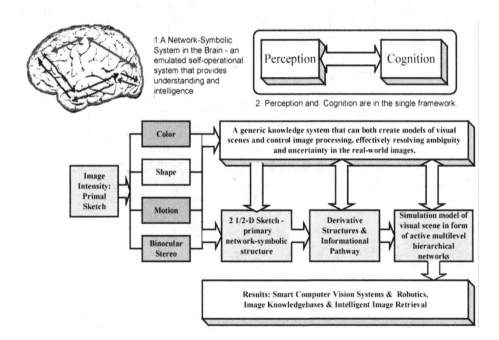

Glossary

Abstraction: A process of separation relational structural component from a particular graph or diagrammatic model that create a Model Space, where nodes do not have assigned implicit symbols.

Active Vision: System that allows Autonomous System to move in the surrounding environment to disambiguate visual information; receives visual information in motion.

Analogy: Synthesis of a new model, using the same structural components but different implicit symbols.

Attention: A mechanism that activates spaces that are relevant to the current situation, activities, and goals.

Autonomous System: Robot or UGV equipped with Cognitive Semiotic Topology device, able to make decisions and conduct actions on its own.

Autonomous System Engine: A Game Engine that allows Autonomous System to play the Game of Life in the real environment.

Blending: Synthesis operation that merges graphs or diagrams in Model Spaces.

Classification: A process of creation a new Symbolic Space: a new Implicit Alphabet, created from a few patterns, based on certain explicit criteria. Such a Space has its own implicit symbol that denotes the concept of Class for the new Alphabet

Cognitive Semiotic Topology: A hierarchical multilevel system consisted of multiple Symbolic and Model Spaces on every level. Symbolic Spaces carry alphabets of implicit symbols that are linked to the nodes of Model Spaces. This separates structural relational components from their labels, allowing structural operations explicitly.

Conceptual Alphabet: A set of unique graph or diagrammatic patterns assigned to the corresponding set of Conceptual Symbols

Conceptual Symbol: A node that represent a graph or diagrammatic pattern on a higher level of system hierarchy.

Context System: Multilevel set of model and symbolic spaces, that helps to disambiguate visual information, and derive model of Scene Graph from Visual Scene.

Egosphere: System of spherical coordinates with the origin in Autonomous System.

Emotions: Positive and negative feedbacks mechanisms.

Game of Life: Set of planned or unplanned actions/moves that allows Autonomous System to survive, and achieve its goals in the real environment.

Generalization: A process of creation a new Symbolic Space: a new Implicit Alphabet artificially created from a few patterns or symbols; or a process of creating a new Model Space, where implicit symbols that label nodes are replaced with implicit symbols of their classes.

Gestalts: Intermediary structures derived from visual information.

Goals: State where the Cognitive Semiotic Topology has enough knowledge that Autonomous System can plan its next steps.

Implicit Alphabet: A set of implicit symbols.

Implicit Symbol: A Perceptual or Conceptual Symbol. Implicit Symbol does not require an explicit semantic labeling as in the semantic networks models. Implicit Symbol denotes certainty in decision, and it is a node on the upper levels of hierarchy.

Knowledge Instinct: A mechanism that drives processes in the Cognitive Semiotic Topology toward reaching goals.

Linker: Mechanism that provides voluntary or an involuntary linking between simultaneously activated nodes.

Model Space: A space that carries a graph or diagrammatic model, in a general sense: a System with a clear structured relational order between the model components.

Network-Symbolic Models: Multilevel hierarchical graph/diagrammatic models, where nodes are labeled with implicit symbols.

Object Buffer: Analogue of human fovea.

Perceptual Alphabet: A recognition device where the set of possible distinctive input patterns are mapped to the corresponded set of Perceptual Symbols

Perceptual Symbol: An output of a recognition mechanism that stands for a recognized input pattern on a higher level of hierarchy.

Scene Graph: Relational graph model that qualitatively describe major components of Visual Scene needed for decision making and action planning, mapped back to Visual Scene.

Set: A few distinctive entities within the same space with no order between the entities

Space: A topological construct that carries an entity. A Space has boundary, which separates that entity from other entities. A Space can be collapsing into a Point on the next level of hierarchy.

Symbol of a Space: Given that a Space may carry a model/system or an alphabet/set, they can have its own implicit symbol that stands for them on a higher level of hierarchy. This collapses a Space into a point, which becomes a Node on the next level of hierarchy. This Symbol stands for the pattern that is bound in the Space.

Symbolic Space: A space that carries an implicit alphabet. This is a set of patterns, and it has no structural part.

Synthesis: A process of creation new graph or diagrammatic models.

System: An ordered graph or diagrammatic model. A System always has some structural part, consisted of linked implicit symbols. System usually has a boundary, and therefore resides within some space.

Understanding: Generated model of relational order that can be used for decision making and action planning.

Visual Buffer: Analogue of primary visual areas, which receive and process visual information from the entire field of vision.

Visual Scene: Visual information of surrounding environment from the real world.

Bibliography

Amosov, N. M. (1967). *Modeling of thinking and the mind*. Spartan Books.

Barsalou, L. W. (1999). Perceptual symbol systems. *Behavioral and Brain Sciences*, 22, 577–660. PMID:11301525

Bezdek, J. C., & Pal, S. K. (1992). *Fuzzy models for pattern recognition: Methods that search for structures in data*. IEEE Press.

Carpenter, G., Grossberg, S., & Rosen, D. B. (1991). Fuzzy ART. *Neural Networks*, 4(6), 759–771. doi:10.1016/0893-6080(91)90056-B

Cherkassky, M. (1998). *Learning from data*. John Wiley & Sons.

Dalen, V. (1991). *Logic and structure*. Springer-Verlag.

Deacon, T. (1997). *The symbolic species*. Academic Press.

Dehaene, S. (2010). Reading in the brain. In A. Loula, R. Gudwin, & J. Queiroz (Eds.), *Artificial Cognition Systems* (pp. 64–105). Hershey, PA: IGI Global.

Dickmanns, E. D. (2007). *Dynamic vision for perception and control of motion*. SBN.

Edelman, G. (1992). *Bright air, brilliant fire*. Basic Books.

Gärdendors, P. (2000). *Conceptual spaces*. Cambridge University Press.

Gersting, J. L. (1999). *Mathematical structures for computer science*. Macmillan.

Glasgow, J., Narayanan, N., & Chandrasekaram, B. (Eds.). (1995). *Diagrammatic reasoning: Cognitive and computational perspectives*. AAAI Press.

Hodges, W. (1997). *A shorter model theory*. Cambridge University Press.

Johnson-Laird, P. N. (1983). *Mental models: Towards a cognitive science of language, inference, and consciousness*. Harvard University Press.

Kohonen, T. (1997). *Self-organizing maps*. Springer.

Lawvere, S. (1997). *Conceptual mathematics*. Cambridge University Press.

Lewin, K. (1994). Continuous symbol systems: The logic of connectionism. In D. S. Levine & M. Aparicio IV, (Eds.), *Neural networks for knowledge representation and inference* (pp. 83–120). Hillsdale, NJ: Lawrence Erlbaum.

MacLennan, B. J. (1994). Continuous computation and the emergence of the discrete. In K. Pribram (Ed.), *Origins: Brain & self-organization* (pp. 121–151). Hillsdale, NJ: Lawrence Erlbaum.

Minsky, M. (1975). A Framework for Representing Knowledge. In P. Winston (Ed.), *The psychology of computer vision*. McGraw-Hill.

Pearl, J. (2000). *Causality*. Cambridge University Press.

Peirce, C. S. (n.d.). *Collected papers of Charles Sanders Peirce* (Vol. 2). Academic Press.

Perlovsky, L. I. (1994). Computational concepts in classification: Neural networks, statistical pattern recognition, and model based vision. *Journal of Mathematical Imaging and Vision*, *4*(1), 81–110. doi:10.1007/BF01250006

Perlovsky, L. I. (1998). Conundrum of combinatorial complexity. *IEEE Trans. PAMI*, *20*(6), 666–670. doi:10.1109/34.683784

Perlovsky, L. I. (2001). *Neural networks, and intellect: Using model based concepts*. New York: Oxford Press.

Perlovsky, L. I. (2007). *Symbols: Integrated cognition and language*. In R. Gudwin & J. Queiroz (Eds.), *Semiotics and intelligent systems development* (pp. 121–151). Hershey, PA: IGI Global. doi:10.4018/978-1-59904-063-9.ch005

Perlovsky, L. I. (2009). Language, and cognition. *Neural Networks*, *22*(3), 247–257. doi:10.1016/j.neunet.2009.03.007 PMID:19419838

Perlovsky, L. I. (2009). Vague-to-crisp neural mechanism of perception. *IEEE Transactions on Neural Networks*, *20*(8), 1363–1367. doi:10.1109/TNN.2009.2025501 PMID:19628456

Perlovsky, L. I. (2011). Abstract concepts in language and cognition, commentary on modeling the cultural evolution of language by Luc Steels. *Physics of Life Reviews*, *8*(4), 375–376. doi:10.1016/j.plrev.2011.10.006 PMID:22036068

Perlovsky, L. I., & Ilin, R. (2010). Grounded symbols in the brain, computational foundations for perceptual symbol system. *Webmed Central Psychology*, *1*(12).

Perlovsky, L. I., & Ilin, R. (2012). Mathematical model of grounded symbols: perceptual symbol system. *Journal of Behavioral and Brain Science*, *2*(2), 195–220. doi:10.4236/jbbs.2012.22024

Perlovsky, L. I., & Kozma, R. (Eds.). (2007). *Neurodynamics of higher-level cognition and consciousness*. Heidelberg, Germany: Springer-Verlag. doi:10.1007/978-3-540-73267-9

Powers, E. J., Gray, D., & Green, R. C. (1996). *Artificial vision: Image description, recognition, and communication*. Academic Press.

Pylyshyn, Z. (1989). *Computation and cognition*. Cambridge, MA: MIT Press.

Rojas, R. (1996). *Neural networks: A systematic approach*. Springer-Verlag.

Shin, S. J. (1994). *The logical status of diagrams*. Cambridge University Press.

Tikhanoff, V., Fontanari, J. F., Cangelosi, A., & Perlovsky, L. I. (2006). Language and cognition integration through modeling field theory: category formation for symbol grounding. Heidelberg, Germany: Springer. doi:10.1007/11840817_40

Tovee, M. J. (1996). *An introduction to visual system*. Cambridge University Press.

Vickers, S. (1989). *Topology via logic*. Cambridge University Press.

Wang, Y. (2008). RTPA: A denotational mathematics for manipulating intelligent and computing behaviors. *International Journal of Cognitive Informatics and Natural Intelligence*, *2*(2), 44–62. doi:10.4018/jcini.2008040103

Related Readings

To continue IGI Global's long-standing tradition of advancing innovation through emerging research, please find below a compiled list of recommended IGI Global book chapters and journal articles in the areas of human-computer interaction, artificial intelligence, and smart environments. These related readings will provide additional information and guidance to further enrich your knowledge and assist you with your own research.

Abdulrahman, M. D., Subramanian, N., Chan, H. K., & Ning, K. (2017). Big Data Analytics: Academic Perspectives. In H. Chan, N. Subramanian, & M. Abdulrahman (Eds.), *Supply Chain Management in the Big Data Era* (pp. 1–12). Hershey, PA: IGI Global. doi:10.4018/978-1-5225-0956-1.ch001

Al-Aiad, A., Alkhatib, K., Al-Ayyad, M., & Hmeidi, I. (2016). A Conceptual Framework of Smart Home Context: An Empirical Investigation. *International Journal of Healthcare Information Systems and Informatics*, 11(3), 42–56. doi:10.4018/IJHISI.2016070103

Almajano, P., Lopez-Sanchez, M., Rodriguez, I., Puig, A., Llorente, M. S., & Ribera, M. (2016). Training Infrastructure to Participate in Real Life Institutions: Learning through Virtual Worlds. In F. Neto, R. de Souza, & A. Gomes (Eds.), *Handbook of Research on 3-D Virtual Environments and Hypermedia for Ubiquitous Learning* (pp. 192–219). Hershey, PA: IGI Global. doi:10.4018/978-1-5225-0125-1.ch008

Ammari, H. M., Shaout, A., & Mustapha, F. (2017). Sensing Coverage in Three-Dimensional Space: A Survey. In N. Ray & A. Turuk (Eds.), *Handbook of Research on Advanced Wireless Sensor Network Applications, Protocols, and Architectures* (pp. 1–28). Hershey, PA: IGI Global. doi:10.4018/978-1-5225-0486-3.ch001

Ang, L., Seng, K. P., & Heng, T. Z. (2016). Information Communication Assistive Technologies for Visually Impaired People. *International Journal of Ambient Computing and Intelligence*, 7(1), 45–68. doi:10.4018/IJACI.2016010103

Ang, R. P., Tan, J. L., Goh, D. H., Huan, V. S., Ooi, Y. P., Boon, J. S., & Fung, D. S. (2017). A Game-Based Approach to Teaching Social Problem-Solving Skills. In R. Zheng & M. Gardner (Eds.), *Handbook of Research on Serious Games for Educational Applications* (pp. 168–195). Hershey, PA: IGI Global. doi:10.4018/978-1-5225-0513-6.ch008

Anthopoulos, L., Janssen, M., & Weerakkody, V. (2016). A Unified Smart City Model (USCM) for Smart City Conceptualization and Benchmarking. *International Journal of Electronic Government Research*, 12(2), 77–93. doi:10.4018/IJEGR.2016040105

Antonova, A. (2017). Preparing for the Forthcoming Industrial Revolution: Beyond Virtual Worlds Technologies for Competence Development and Learning. *International Journal of Virtual and Augmented Reality*, 1(1), 16–28. doi:10.4018/IJVAR.2017010102

Applin, S. A., & Fischer, M. D. (2017). Thing Theory: Connecting Humans to Smart Healthcare. In C. Reis & M. Maximiano (Eds.), *Internet of Things and Advanced Application in Healthcare* (pp. 249–265). Hershey, PA: IGI Global. doi:10.4018/978-1-5225-1820-4.ch009

Armstrong, S., & Yampolskiy, R. V. (2017). Security Solutions for Intelligent and Complex Systems. In M. Dawson, M. Eltayeb, & M. Omar (Eds.), *Security Solutions for Hyperconnectivity and the Internet of Things* (pp. 37–88). Hershey, PA: IGI Global. doi:10.4018/978-1-5225-0741-3.ch003

Auza, J. M., & de Marca, J. R. (2017). A Mobility Model for Crowd Sensing Simulation. *International Journal of Interdisciplinary Telecommunications and Networking*, 9(1), 14–25. doi:10.4018/IJITN.2017010102

Ayesh, A., Arevalillo-Herráez, M., & Ferri, F. J. (2016). Towards Psychologically based Personalised Modelling of Emotions Using Associative Classifiers. *International Journal of Cognitive Informatics and Natural Intelligence*, *10*(2), 52–64. doi:10.4018/IJCINI.2016040103

Badilla, G. L., & Gaynor, J. M. (2017). Analysis of New Opotoelectronic Device for Detection of Heavy Metals in Corroded Soils: Design a Novel Optoelectronic Devices. In O. Sergiyenko & J. Rodriguez-Quiñonez (Eds.), *Developing and Applying Optoelectronics in Machine Vision* (pp. 273–302). Hershey, PA: IGI Global. doi:10.4018/978-1-5225-0632-4.ch009

Balas, C. E. (2016). An Artificial Neural Network Model as the Decision Support System of Ports. In E. Ocalir-Akunal (Ed.), *Using Decision Support Systems for Transportation Planning Efficiency* (pp. 36–60). Hershey, PA: IGI Global. doi:10.4018/978-1-4666-8648-9.ch002

Barbeito, A., Painho, M., Cabral, P., & ONeill, J. G. (2017). Beyond Digital Human Body Atlases: Segmenting an Integrated 3D Topological Model of the Human Body. *International Journal of E-Health and Medical Communications*, *8*(1), 19–36. doi:10.4018/IJEHMC.2017010102

Berrahal, S., & Boudriga, N. (2017). The Risks of Wearable Technologies to Individuals and Organizations. In A. Marrington, D. Kerr, & J. Gammack (Eds.), *Managing Security Issues and the Hidden Dangers of Wearable Technologies* (pp. 18–46). Hershey, PA: IGI Global. doi:10.4018/978-1-5225-1016-1.ch002

Bhargavi, P., Jyothi, S., & Mamatha, D. M. (2017). A Study on Hybridization of Intelligent Techniques in Bioinformatics. In S. Bhattacharyya, S. De, I. Pan, & P. Dutta (Eds.), *Intelligent Multidimensional Data Clustering and Analysis* (pp. 358–379). Hershey, PA: IGI Global. doi:10.4018/978-1-5225-1776-4.ch014

Bhattacharya, S. (2017). A Predictive Linear Regression Model for Affective State Detection of Mobile Touch Screen Users. *International Journal of Mobile Human Computer Interaction*, *9*(1), 30–44. doi:10.4018/IJMHCI.2017010103

Biagi, L., Comai, S., Mangiarotti, R., Matteucci, M., Negretti, M., & Yavuz, S. U. (2017). Enriching Geographic Maps with Accessible Paths Derived from Implicit Mobile Device Data Collection. In S. Konomi & G. Roussos (Eds.), *Enriching Urban Spaces with Ambient Computing, the Internet of Things, and Smart City Design* (pp. 89–113). Hershey, PA: IGI Global. doi:10.4018/978-1-5225-0827-4.ch005

Bogatinov, D. S., Bogdanoski, M., & Angelevski, S. (2016). AI-Based Cyber Defense for More Secure Cyberspace. In M. Hadji-Janev & M. Bogdanoski (Eds.), *Handbook of Research on Civil Society and National Security in the Era of Cyber Warfare* (pp. 220–237). Hershey, PA: IGI Global. doi:10.4018/978-1-4666-8793-6.ch011

Bottrighi, A., Leonardi, G., Piovesan, L., & Terenziani, P. (2016). Knowledge-Based Support to the Treatment of Exceptions in Computer Interpretable Clinical Guidelines. *International Journal of Knowledge-Based Organizations*, 6(3), 1–27. doi:10.4018/IJKBO.2016070101

Bureš, V., Tučník, P., Mikulecký, P., Mls, K., & Blecha, P. (2016). Application of Ambient Intelligence in Educational Institutions: Visions and Architectures. *International Journal of Ambient Computing and Intelligence*, 7(1), 94–120. doi:10.4018/IJACI.2016010105

Castellet, A. (2016). What If Devices Take Command: Content Innovation Perspectives for Smart Wearables in the Mobile Ecosystem. *International Journal of Handheld Computing Research*, 7(2), 16–33. doi:10.4018/IJHCR.2016040102

Champaty, B., Ray, S. S., Mohapatra, B., & Pal, K. (2017). Voluntary Blink Controlled Communication Protocol for Bed-Ridden Patients. In N. Kamila (Ed.), *Handbook of Research on Wireless Sensor Network Trends, Technologies, and Applications* (pp. 162–195). Hershey, PA: IGI Global. doi:10.4018/978-1-5225-0501-3.ch008

Chawla, S. (2017). Multi-Agent-Based Information Retrieval System Using Information Scent in Query Log Mining for Effective Web Search. In G. Sreedhar (Ed.), *Web Data Mining and the Development of Knowledge-Based Decision Support Systems* (pp. 131–156). Hershey, PA: IGI Global. doi:10.4018/978-1-5225-1877-8.ch008

Chen, G., Wang, E., Sun, X., & Lu, Y. (2016). An Intelligent Approval System for City Construction based on Cloud Computing and Big Data. *International Journal of Grid and High Performance Computing, 8*(3), 57–69. doi:10.4018/IJGHPC.2016070104

Cointault, F., Han, S., Rabatel, G., Jay, S., Rousseau, D., Billiot, B., & Salon, C. et al. (2017). 3D Imaging Systems for Agricultural Applications: Characterization of Crop and Root Phenotyping. In O. Sergiyenko & J. Rodriguez-Quiñonez (Eds.), *Developing and Applying Optoelectronics in Machine Vision* (pp. 236–272). Hershey, PA: IGI Global. doi:10.4018/978-1-5225-0632-4.ch008

Connor, A. M. (2016). A Historical Review of Creative Technologies. In A. Connor & S. Marks (Eds.), *Creative Technologies for Multidisciplinary Applications* (pp. 1–24). Hershey, PA: IGI Global. doi:10.4018/978-1-5225-0016-2.ch001

Connor, A. M., Sosa, R., Karmokar, S., Marks, S., Buxton, M., Gribble, A. M., & Foottit, J. et al. (2016). Exposing Core Competencies for Future Creative Technologists. In A. Connor & S. Marks (Eds.), *Creative Technologies for Multidisciplinary Applications* (pp. 377–397). Hershey, PA: IGI Global. doi:10.4018/978-1-5225-0016-2.ch015

Cook, A. E., & Wei, W. (2017). Using Eye Movements to Study Reading Processes: Methodological Considerations. In C. Was, F. Sansosti, & B. Morris (Eds.), *Eye-Tracking Technology Applications in Educational Research* (pp. 27–47). Hershey, PA: IGI Global. doi:10.4018/978-1-5225-1005-5.ch002

Corradini, A., & Mehta, M. (2016). A Graphical Tool for the Creation of Behaviors in Virtual Worlds. In J. Turner, M. Nixon, U. Bernardet, & S. DiPaola (Eds.), *Integrating Cognitive Architectures into Virtual Character Design* (pp. 65–93). Hershey, PA: IGI Global. doi:10.4018/978-1-5225-0454-2.ch003

Corrêa, L. D., & Dorn, M. (2017). Multi-Agent Systems in Three-Dimensional Protein Structure Prediction. In D. Adamatti (Ed.), *Multi-Agent-Based Simulations Applied to Biological and Environmental Systems* (pp. 241–278). Hershey, PA: IGI Global. doi:10.4018/978-1-5225-1756-6.ch011

Croatti, A., Ricci, A., & Viroli, M. (2017). Towards a Mobile Augmented Reality System for Emergency Management: The Case of SAFE. *International Journal of Distributed Systems and Technologies, 8*(1), 46–58. doi:10.4018/IJDST.2017010104

Dafer, M., & El-Abed, M. (2017). Evaluation of Keystroke Dynamics Authentication Systems: Analysis of Physical and Touch Screen Keyboards. In M. Dawson, D. Kisku, P. Gupta, J. Sing, & W. Li (Eds.), *Developing Next-Generation Countermeasures for Homeland Security Threat Prevention* (pp. 306–329). Hershey, PA: IGI Global. doi:10.4018/978-1-5225-0703-1.ch014

Das, P. K., Ghosh, D., Jagtap, P., Joshi, A., & Finin, T. (2017). Preserving User Privacy and Security in Context-Aware Mobile Platforms. In S. Mukherjea (Ed.), *Mobile Application Development, Usability, and Security* (pp. 166–193). Hershey, PA: IGI Global. doi:10.4018/978-1-5225-0945-5.ch008

De Filippi, F., Coscia, C., & Guido, R. (2017). How Technologies Can Enhance Open Policy Making and Citizen-Responsive Urban Planning: MiraMap - A Governing Tool for the Mirafiori Sud District in Turin (Italy). *International Journal of E-Planning Research, 6*(1), 23–42. doi:10.4018/IJEPR.2017010102

De Pasquale, D., Wood, E., Gottardo, A., Jones, J. A., Kaplan, R., & DeMarco, A. (2017). Tracking Children's Interactions with Traditional Text and Computer-Based Early Literacy Media. In C. Was, F. Sansosti, & B. Morris (Eds.), *Eye-Tracking Technology Applications in Educational Research* (pp. 107–121). Hershey, PA: IGI Global. doi:10.4018/978-1-5225-1005-5.ch006

Del Fiore, G., Mainetti, L., Mighali, V., Patrono, L., Alletto, S., Cucchiara, R., & Serra, G. (2016). A Location-Aware Architecture for an IoT-Based Smart Museum. *International Journal of Electronic Government Research, 12*(2), 39–55. doi:10.4018/IJEGR.2016040103

Desjarlais, M. (2017). The Use of Eye-gaze to Understand Multimedia Learning. In C. Was, F. Sansosti, & B. Morris (Eds.), *Eye-Tracking Technology Applications in Educational Research* (pp. 122–142). Hershey, PA: IGI Global. doi:10.4018/978-1-5225-1005-5.ch007

Diviacco, P., & Leadbetter, A. (2017). Balancing Formalization and Representation in Cross-Domain Data Management for Sustainable Development. In P. Diviacco, A. Leadbetter, & H. Glaves (Eds.), *Oceanographic and Marine Cross-Domain Data Management for Sustainable Development* (pp. 23–46). Hershey, PA: IGI Global. doi:10.4018/978-1-5225-0700-0.ch002

Dragoicea, M., Falcao e Cunha, J., Alexandru, M. V., & Constantinescu, D. A. (2017). Modelling and Simulation Perspective in Service Design: Experience in Transport Information Service Development. In S. Rozenes & Y. Cohen (Eds.), *Handbook of Research on Strategic Alliances and Value Co-Creation in the Service Industry* (pp. 374–399). Hershey, PA: IGI Global. doi:10.4018/978-1-5225-2084-9.ch019

El Khayat, G. A., & Fashal, N. A. (2017). Inter and Intra Cities Smartness: A Survey on Location Problems and GIS Tools. In S. Faiz & K. Mahmoudi (Eds.), *Handbook of Research on Geographic Information Systems Applications and Advancements* (pp. 296–320). Hershey, PA: IGI Global. doi:10.4018/978-1-5225-0937-0.ch011

Eteme, A. A., & Ngossaha, J. M. (2017). Urban Master Data Management: Case of the YUSIIP Platform. In S. Faiz & K. Mahmoudi (Eds.), *Handbook of Research on Geographic Information Systems Applications and Advancements* (pp. 441–465). Hershey, PA: IGI Global. doi:10.4018/978-1-5225-0937-0.ch018

Fisher, K. J., Nichols, T., Isbister, K., & Fuller, T. (2017). Quantifying "Magic": Creating Good Player Experiences on Xbox Kinect. In B. Dubbels (Ed.), *Transforming Gaming and Computer Simulation Technologies across Industries* (pp. 1–16). Hershey, PA: IGI Global. doi:10.4018/978-1-5225-1817-4.ch001

Flores-Fuentes, W., Rivas-Lopez, M., Hernandez-Balbuena, D., Sergiyenko, O., Rodríguez-Quiñonez, J. C., Rivera-Castillo, J., & Basaca-Preciado, L. C. et al. (2017). Applying Optoelectronic Devices Fusion in Machine Vision: Spatial Coordinate Measurement. In O. Sergiyenko & J. Rodriguez-Quiñonez (Eds.), *Developing and Applying Optoelectronics in Machine Vision* (pp. 1–37). Hershey, PA: IGI Global. doi:10.4018/978-1-5225-0632-4.ch001

Forti, I. (2017). A Cross Reading of Landscape through Digital Landscape Models: The Case of Southern Garda. In A. Ippolito (Ed.), *Handbook of Research on Emerging Technologies for Architectural and Archaeological Heritage* (pp. 532–561). Hershey, PA: IGI Global. doi:10.4018/978-1-5225-0675-1.ch018

Gammack, J., & Marrington, A. (2017). The Promise and Perils of Wearable Technologies. In A. Marrington, D. Kerr, & J. Gammack (Eds.), *Managing Security Issues and the Hidden Dangers of Wearable Technologies* (pp. 1–17). Hershey, PA: IGI Global. doi:10.4018/978-1-5225-1016-1.ch001

Ghaffarianhoseini, A., Ghaffarianhoseini, A., Tookey, J., Omrany, H., Fleury, A., Naismith, N., & Ghaffarianhoseini, M. (2016). The Essence of Smart Homes: Application of Intelligent Technologies towards Smarter Urban Future. In A. Connor & S. Marks (Eds.), *Creative Technologies for Multidisciplinary Applications* (pp. 334–376). Hershey, PA: IGI Global. doi:10.4018/978-1-5225-0016-2.ch014

Gharbi, A., De Runz, C., & Akdag, H. (2017). Urban Development Modelling: A Survey. In S. Faiz & K. Mahmoudi (Eds.), *Handbook of Research on Geographic Information Systems Applications and Advancements* (pp. 96–124). Hershey, PA: IGI Global. doi:10.4018/978-1-5225-0937-0.ch004

Ghosh, S., Mitra, S., Ghosh, S., & Chakraborty, S. (2017). Seismic Reliability Analysis in the Framework of Metamodelling Based Monte Carlo Simulation. In P. Samui, S. Chakraborty, & D. Kim (Eds.), *Modeling and Simulation Techniques in Structural Engineering* (pp. 192–208). Hershey, PA: IGI Global. doi:10.4018/978-1-5225-0588-4.ch006

Guesgen, H. W., & Marsland, S. (2016). Using Contextual Information for Recognising Human Behaviour. *International Journal of Ambient Computing and Intelligence*, 7(1), 27–44. doi:10.4018/IJACI.2016010102

Hameur Laine, A., & Brahimi, S. (2017). Background on Context-Aware Computing Systems. In C. Reis & M. Maximiano (Eds.), *Internet of Things and Advanced Application in Healthcare* (pp. 1–31). Hershey, PA: IGI Global. doi:10.4018/978-1-5225-1820-4.ch001

Harrati, N., Bouchrika, I., Mahfouf, Z., & Ladjailia, A. (2017). Evaluation Methods for E-Learning Applications in Terms of User Satisfaction and Interface Usability. In P. Vu, S. Fredrickson, & C. Moore (Eds.), *Handbook of Research on Innovative Pedagogies and Technologies for Online Learning in Higher Education* (pp. 427–448). Hershey, PA: IGI Global. doi:10.4018/978-1-5225-1851-8.ch018

Harwood, T. (2016). Machinima: A Meme of Our Time. In A. Connor & S. Marks (Eds.), *Creative Technologies for Multidisciplinary Applications* (pp. 149–181). Hershey, PA: IGI Global. doi:10.4018/978-1-5225-0016-2.ch007

Hassani, K., & Lee, W. (2016). A Universal Architecture for Migrating Cognitive Agents: A Case Study on Automatic Animation Generation. In J. Turner, M. Nixon, U. Bernardet, & S. DiPaola (Eds.), *Integrating Cognitive Architectures into Virtual Character Design* (pp. 238–265). Hershey, PA: IGI Global. doi:10.4018/978-1-5225-0454-2.ch009

Herpich, F., Nunes, F. B., Voss, G. B., & Medina, R. D. (2016). Three-Dimensional Virtual Environment and NPC: A Perspective about Intelligent Agents Ubiquitous. In F. Neto, R. de Souza, & A. Gomes (Eds.), *Handbook of Research on 3-D Virtual Environments and Hypermedia for Ubiquitous Learning* (pp. 510–536). Hershey, PA: IGI Global. doi:10.4018/978-1-5225-0125-1.ch021

Higgins, C., Kearns, Á., Ryan, C., & Fernstrom, M. (2016). The Role of Gamification and Evolutionary Computation in the Provision of Self-Guided Speech Therapy. In D. Novák, B. Tulu, & H. Brendryen (Eds.), *Handbook of Research on Holistic Perspectives in Gamification for Clinical Practice* (pp. 158–182). Hershey, PA: IGI Global. doi:10.4018/978-1-4666-9522-1.ch008

Honarvar, A. R., & Sami, A. (2016). Extracting Usage Patterns from Power Usage Data of Homes Appliances in Smart Home using Big Data Platform. *International Journal of Information Technology and Web Engineering*, *11*(2), 39–50. doi:10.4018/IJITWE.2016040103

Hulsey, N. (2016). Between Games and Simulation: Gamification and Convergence in Creative Computing. In A. Connor & S. Marks (Eds.), *Creative Technologies for Multidisciplinary Applications* (pp. 130–148). Hershey, PA: IGI Global. doi:10.4018/978-1-5225-0016-2.ch006

Ion, A., & Patrascu, M. (2017). Agent Based Modelling of Smart Structures: The Challenges of a New Research Domain. In P. Samui, S. Chakraborty, & D. Kim (Eds.), *Modeling and Simulation Techniques in Structural Engineering* (pp. 38–60). Hershey, PA: IGI Global. doi:10.4018/978-1-5225-0588-4.ch002

Iyawe, B. I. (2017). User Performance Testing Indicator: User Performance Indicator Tool (UPIT). In S. Saeed, Y. Bamarouf, T. Ramayah, & S. Iqbal (Eds.), *Design Solutions for User-Centric Information Systems* (pp. 205–229). Hershey, PA: IGI Global. doi:10.4018/978-1-5225-1944-7.ch012

Izumi, S., Hata, M., Takahira, H., Soylu, M., Edo, A., Abe, T., & Suganuma, T. (2017). A Proposal of SDN Based Disaster-Aware Smart Routing for Highly-Available Information Storage Systems and Its Evaluation. *International Journal of Software Science and Computational Intelligence, 9*(1), 68–82. doi:10.4018/IJSSCI.2017010105

Jarušek, R., & Kocian, V. (2017). Artificial Intelligence Algorithms for Classification and Pattern Recognition. In E. Volna, M. Kotyrba, & M. Janosek (Eds.), *Pattern Recognition and Classification in Time Series Data* (pp. 53–85). Hershey, PA: IGI Global. doi:10.4018/978-1-5225-0565-5.ch003

Jayabalan, J., Yildirim, D., Kim, D., & Samui, P. (2017). Design Optimization of a Wind Turbine Using Artificial Intelligence. In M. Ram & J. Davim (Eds.), *Mathematical Concepts and Applications in Mechanical Engineering and Mechatronics* (pp. 38–66). Hershey, PA: IGI Global. doi:10.4018/978-1-5225-1639-2.ch003

Jena, G. C. (2017). Multi-Sensor Data Fusion (MSDF). In N. Ray & A. Turuk (Eds.), *Handbook of Research on Advanced Wireless Sensor Network Applications, Protocols, and Architectures* (pp. 29–61). Hershey, PA: IGI Global. doi:10.4018/978-1-5225-0486-3.ch002

Kale, G. V., & Patil, V. H. (2016). A Study of Vision based Human Motion Recognition and Analysis. *International Journal of Ambient Computing and Intelligence, 7*(2), 75–92. doi:10.4018/IJACI.2016070104

Kasemsap, K. (2017). Mastering Intelligent Decision Support Systems in Enterprise Information Management. In G. Sreedhar (Ed.), *Web Data Mining and the Development of Knowledge-Based Decision Support Systems* (pp. 35–56). Hershey, PA: IGI Global. doi:10.4018/978-1-5225-1877-8.ch004

Kim, S. (2017). New Game Paradigm for IoT Systems. In *Game Theory Solutions for the Internet of Things: Emerging Research and Opportunities* (pp. 101–147). Hershey, PA: IGI Global. doi:10.4018/978-1-5225-1952-2. ch004

Ladjailia, A., Bouchrika, I., Harrati, N., & Mahfouf, Z. (2017). Encoding Human Motion for Automated Activity Recognition in Surveillance Applications. In N. Dey, A. Ashour, & S. Acharjee (Eds.), *Applied Video Processing in Surveillance and Monitoring Systems* (pp. 170–192). Hershey, PA: IGI Global. doi:10.4018/978-1-5225-1022-2.ch008

Lanza, J., Sotres, P., Sánchez, L., Galache, J. A., Santana, J. R., Gutiérrez, V., & Muñoz, L. (2016). Managing Large Amounts of Data Generated by a Smart City Internet of Things Deployment. *International Journal on Semantic Web and Information Systems*, *12*(4), 22–42. doi:10.4018/IJSWIS.2016100102

Lee, H. (2017). The Internet of Things and Assistive Technologies for People with Disabilities: Applications, Trends, and Issues. In C. Reis & M. Maximiano (Eds.), *Internet of Things and Advanced Application in Healthcare* (pp. 32–65). Hershey, PA: IGI Global. doi:10.4018/978-1-5225-1820-4.ch002

Li, W. H., Zhu, K., & Fu, H. (2017). Exploring the Design Space of Bezel-Initiated Gestures for Mobile Interaction. *International Journal of Mobile Human Computer Interaction*, *9*(1), 16–29. doi:10.4018/IJMHCI.2017010102

Ludwig, T., Kotthaus, C., & Pipek, V. (2015). Should I Try Turning It Off and On Again?: Outlining HCI Challenges for Cyber-Physical Production Systems. *International Journal of Information Systems for Crisis Response and Management*, *7*(3), 55–68. doi:10.4018/ijiscram.2015070104

Luo, L., Kiewra, K. A., Peteranetz, M. S., & Flanigan, A. E. (2017). Using Eye-Tracking Technology to Understand How Graphic Organizers Aid Student Learning. In C. Was, F. Sansosti, & B. Morris (Eds.), *Eye-Tracking Technology Applications in Educational Research* (pp. 220–238). Hershey, PA: IGI Global. doi:10.4018/978-1-5225-1005-5.ch011

Mahanty, R., & Mahanti, P. K. (2016). Unleashing Artificial Intelligence onto Big Data: A Review. In S. Dash & B. Subudhi (Eds.), *Handbook of Research on Computational Intelligence Applications in Bioinformatics* (pp. 1–16). Hershey, PA: IGI Global. doi:10.4018/978-1-5225-0427-6.ch001

Marzuki, A. (2017). CMOS Image Sensor: Analog and Mixed-Signal Circuits. In O. Sergiyenko & J. Rodriguez-Quiñonez (Eds.), *Developing and Applying Optoelectronics in Machine Vision* (pp. 38–78). Hershey, PA: IGI Global. doi:10.4018/978-1-5225-0632-4.ch002

McKenna, H. P. (2017). Urbanizing the Ambient: Why People Matter So Much in Smart Cities. In S. Konomi & G. Roussos (Eds.), *Enriching Urban Spaces with Ambient Computing, the Internet of Things, and Smart City Design* (pp. 209–231). Hershey, PA: IGI Global. doi:10.4018/978-1-5225-0827-4.ch011

Meghanathan, N. (2017). Diameter-Aggregation Delay Tradeoff for Data Gathering Trees in Wireless Sensor Networks. In N. Kamila (Ed.), *Handbook of Research on Wireless Sensor Network Trends, Technologies, and Applications* (pp. 237–253). Hershey, PA: IGI Global. doi:10.4018/978-1-5225-0501-3.ch010

Moein, S. (2014). Artificial Intelligence in Medical Science. In *Medical Diagnosis Using Artificial Neural Networks* (pp. 11–23). Hershey, PA: IGI Global. doi:10.4018/978-1-4666-6146-2.ch002

Moein, S. (2014). Artificial Neural Network for Medical Diagnosis. In *Medical Diagnosis Using Artificial Neural Networks* (pp. 85–94). Hershey, PA: IGI Global. doi:10.4018/978-1-4666-6146-2.ch007

Moein, S. (2014). Types of Artificial Neural Network. In *Medical Diagnosis Using Artificial Neural Networks* (pp. 58–67). Hershey, PA: IGI Global. doi:10.4018/978-1-4666-6146-2.ch005

Moser, S. (2017). Linking Virtual and Real-life Environments: Scrutinizing Ubiquitous Learning Scenarios. In S. Şad & M. Ebner (Eds.), *Digital Tools for Seamless Learning* (pp. 214–239). Hershey, PA: IGI Global. doi:10.4018/978-1-5225-1692-7.ch011

Mumini, O. O., Adebisi, F. M., Edward, O. O., & Abidemi, A. S. (2016). Simulation of Stock Prediction System using Artificial Neural Networks. *International Journal of Business Analytics*, *3*(3), 25–44. doi:10.4018/IJBAN.2016070102

Muñoz, M. C., & Moh, M. (2017). Authentication of Smart Grid: The Case for Using Merkle Trees. In M. Ferrag & A. Ahmim (Eds.), *Security Solutions and Applied Cryptography in Smart Grid Communications* (pp. 117–136). Hershey, PA: IGI Global. doi:10.4018/978-1-5225-1829-7.ch007

Mushcab, H., Kernohan, W. G., Wallace, J., Harper, R., & Martin, S. (2017). Self-Management of Diabetes Mellitus with Remote Monitoring: A Retrospective Review of 214 Cases. *International Journal of E-Health and Medical Communications*, 8(1), 52–61. doi:10.4018/IJEHMC.2017010104

Mutlu-Bayraktar, D. (2017). Usability Evaluation of Social Media Web Sites and Applications via Eye-Tracking Method. In S. Hai-Jew (Ed.), *Social Media Data Extraction and Content Analysis* (pp. 85–112). Hershey, PA: IGI Global. doi:10.4018/978-1-5225-0648-5.ch004

Nadler, S. (2017). Mobile Location Tracking: Indoor and Outdoor Location Tracking. In S. Mukherjea (Ed.), *Mobile Application Development, Usability, and Security* (pp. 194–209). Hershey, PA: IGI Global. doi:10.4018/978-1-5225-0945-5.ch009

Nagpal, R., Mehrotra, D., & Bhatia, P. K. (2017). The State of Art in Website Usability Evaluation Methods. In S. Saeed, Y. Bamarouf, T. Ramayah, & S. Iqbal (Eds.), *Design Solutions for User-Centric Information Systems* (pp. 275–296). Hershey, PA: IGI Global. doi:10.4018/978-1-5225-1944-7.ch015

Nava, J., & Osorio, A. (2016). A Hybrid Intelligent Risk Identification Model for Configuration Management in Aerospace Systems. In A. Ochoa-Zezzatti, J. Sánchez, M. Cedillo-Campos, & M. de Lourdes (Eds.), *Handbook of Research on Military, Aeronautical, and Maritime Logistics and Operations* (pp. 319–345). Hershey, PA: IGI Global. doi:10.4018/978-1-4666-9779-9.ch017

Nazareth, A., Odean, R., & Pruden, S. M. (2017). The Use of Eye-Tracking in Spatial Thinking Research. In C. Was, F. Sansosti, & B. Morris (Eds.), *Eye-Tracking Technology Applications in Educational Research* (pp. 239–260). Hershey, PA: IGI Global. doi:10.4018/978-1-5225-1005-5.ch012

Neves, J., Zeleznikow, J., & Vicente, H. (2016). Quality of Judgment Assessment. In P. Novais & D. Carneiro (Eds.), *Interdisciplinary Perspectives on Contemporary Conflict Resolution* (pp. 96–110). Hershey, PA: IGI Global. doi:10.4018/978-1-5225-0245-6.ch006

Niewiadomski, R., & Anderson, D. (2017). The Rise of Artificial Intelligence: Its Impact on Labor Market and Beyond. In R. Batko & A. Szopa (Eds.), *Strategic Imperatives and Core Competencies in the Era of Robotics and Artificial Intelligence* (pp. 29–49). Hershey, PA: IGI Global. doi:10.4018/978-1-5225-1656-9.ch003

Nishani, L., & Biba, M. (2017). Statistical Relational Learning for Collaborative Filtering a State-of-the-Art Review. In V. Bhatnagar (Ed.), *Collaborative Filtering Using Data Mining and Analysis* (pp. 250–269). Hershey, PA: IGI Global. doi:10.4018/978-1-5225-0489-4.ch014

Ogata, T. (2016). Computational and Cognitive Approaches to Narratology from the Perspective of Narrative Generation. In T. Ogata & T. Akimoto (Eds.), *Computational and Cognitive Approaches to Narratology* (pp. 1–74). Hershey, PA: IGI Global. doi:10.4018/978-1-5225-0432-0.ch001

Ozpinar, A., & Kucukasci, E. S. (2016). Use of Chaotic Randomness Numbers: Metaheuristic and Artificial Intelligence Algorithms. In N. Celebi (Ed.), *Intelligent Techniques for Data Analysis in Diverse Settings* (pp. 207–227). Hershey, PA: IGI Global. doi:10.4018/978-1-5225-0075-9.ch010

Ozpinar, A., & Ozil, E. (2016). Smart Grid and Demand Side Management: Application of Metaheuristic and Artificial Intelligence Algorithms. In A. Ahmad & N. Hassan (Eds.), *Smart Grid as a Solution for Renewable and Efficient Energy* (pp. 49–68). Hershey, PA: IGI Global. doi:10.4018/978-1-5225-0072-8.ch003

Papadopoulos, H. (2016). Designing Smart Home Environments for Unobtrusive Monitoring for Independent Living: The Use Case of USEFIL. *International Journal of E-Services and Mobile Applications*, 8(1), 47–63. doi:10.4018/IJESMA.2016010104

Papadopoulos, H. (2016). Modeling Place: Usage of Mobile Data Services and Applications within Different Places. *International Journal of E-Services and Mobile Applications*, 8(2), 1–20. doi:10.4018/IJESMA.2016040101

Parey, A., & Ahuja, A. S. (2016). Application of Artificial Intelligence to Gearbox Fault Diagnosis: A Review. In S. John (Ed.), *Handbook of Research on Generalized and Hybrid Set Structures and Applications for Soft Computing* (pp. 536–562). Hershey, PA: IGI Global. doi:10.4018/978-1-4666-9798-0.ch024

Parikh, C. (2017). Eye-Tracking Technology: A Closer Look at Eye-Tracking Paradigms with High-Risk Populations. In C. Was, F. Sansosti, & B. Morris (Eds.), *Eye-Tracking Technology Applications in Educational Research* (pp. 283–302). Hershey, PA: IGI Global. doi:10.4018/978-1-5225-1005-5.ch014

Peng, M., Qin, Y., Tang, C., & Deng, X. (2016). An E-Commerce Customer Service Robot Based on Intention Recognition Model. *Journal of Electronic Commerce in Organizations, 14*(1), 34–44. doi:10.4018/JECO.2016010104

Pessoa, C. R., & Júnior, M. D. (2017). A Telecommunications Approach in Systems for Effective Logistics and Supply Chains. In G. Jamil, A. Soares, & C. Pessoa (Eds.), *Handbook of Research on Information Management for Effective Logistics and Supply Chains* (pp. 437–452). Hershey, PA: IGI Global. doi:10.4018/978-1-5225-0973-8.ch023

Pineda, R. G. (2016). Where the Interaction Is Not: Reflections on the Philosophy of Human-Computer Interaction. *International Journal of Art, Culture and Design Technologies, 5*(1), 1–12. doi:10.4018/IJACDT.2016010101

Poitras, E. G., Harley, J. M., Compeau, T., Kee, K., & Lajoie, S. P. (2017). Augmented Reality in Informal Learning Settings: Leveraging Technology for the Love of History. In R. Zheng & M. Gardner (Eds.), *Handbook of Research on Serious Games for Educational Applications* (pp. 272–293). Hershey, PA: IGI Global. doi:10.4018/978-1-5225-0513-6.ch013

Powell, W. A., Corbett, N., & Powell, V. (2016). The Rise of the Virtual Human. In A. Connor & S. Marks (Eds.), *Creative Technologies for Multidisciplinary Applications* (pp. 99–129). Hershey, PA: IGI Global. doi:10.4018/978-1-5225-0016-2.ch005

Prakash, L. S., & Saini, D. K. (2017). Instructional Design Technology in Higher Education System: Role and Impact on Developing Creative Learning Environments. In C. Zhou (Ed.), *Handbook of Research on Creative Problem-Solving Skill Development in Higher Education* (pp. 378–406). Hershey, PA: IGI Global. doi:10.4018/978-1-5225-0643-0.ch017

Rahmani, M. E., Amine, A., & Hamou, R. M. (2016). Supervised Machine Learning for Plants Identification Based on Images of Their Leaves. *International Journal of Agricultural and Environmental Information Systems*, 7(4), 17–31. doi:10.4018/IJAEIS.2016100102

Ramanathan, U. (2017). How Smart Operations Help Better Planning and Replenishment?: Empirical Study – Supply Chain Collaboration for Smart Operations. In H. Chan, N. Subramanian, & M. Abdulrahman (Eds.), *Supply Chain Management in the Big Data Era* (pp. 25–49). Hershey, PA: IGI Global. doi:10.4018/978-1-5225-0956-1.ch003

Rao, M., & Kamila, N. K. (2017). Target Tracking in Wireless Sensor Network: The Current State of Art. In N. Kamila (Ed.), *Handbook of Research on Wireless Sensor Network Trends, Technologies, and Applications* (pp. 413–437). Hershey, PA: IGI Global. doi:10.4018/978-1-5225-0501-3.ch017

Rappaport, J. M., Richter, S. B., & Kennedy, D. T. (2016). A Strategic Perspective on Using Symbolic Transformation in STEM Education: Robotics and Automation. *International Journal of Strategic Decision Sciences*, 7(1), 39–75. doi:10.4018/IJSDS.2016010103

Rashid, E. (2016). R4 Model for Case-Based Reasoning and Its Application for Software Fault Prediction. *International Journal of Software Science and Computational Intelligence*, 8(3), 19–38. doi:10.4018/IJSSCI.2016070102

Rathore, M. M., Paul, A., Ahmad, A., & Jeon, G. (2017). IoT-Based Big Data: From Smart City towards Next Generation Super City Planning. *International Journal on Semantic Web and Information Systems*, 13(1), 28–47. doi:10.4018/IJSWIS.2017010103

Reeberg de Mello, A., & Stemmer, M. R. (2017). Automated Visual Inspection System for Printed Circuit Boards for Small Series Production: A Multiagent Context Approach. In O. Sergiyenko & J. Rodriguez-Quiñonez (Eds.), *Developing and Applying Optoelectronics in Machine Vision* (pp. 79–107). Hershey, PA: IGI Global. doi:10.4018/978-1-5225-0632-4.ch003

Rodrigues, P., & Rosa, P. J. (2017). Eye-Tracking as a Research Methodology in Educational Context: A Spanning Framework. In C. Was, F. Sansosti, & B. Morris (Eds.), *Eye-Tracking Technology Applications in Educational Research* (pp. 1–26). Hershey, PA: IGI Global. doi:10.4018/978-1-5225-1005-5.ch001

Rosen, Y., & Mosharraf, M. (2016). Computer Agent Technologies in Collaborative Assessments. In Y. Rosen, S. Ferrara, & M. Mosharraf (Eds.), *Handbook of Research on Technology Tools for Real-World Skill Development* (pp. 319–343). Hershey, PA: IGI Global. doi:10.4018/978-1-4666-9441-5.ch012

Rosenzweig, E. D., & Bendoly, E. (2017). An Investigation of Competitor Networks in Manufacturing Strategy and Implications for Performance. In A. Vlachvei, O. Notta, K. Karantininis, & N. Tsounis (Eds.), *Factors Affecting Firm Competitiveness and Performance in the Modern Business World* (pp. 43–82). Hershey, PA: IGI Global. doi:10.4018/978-1-5225-0843-4.ch002

S., J. R., & Omman, B. (2017). A Technical Assessment on License Plate Detection System. In M. S., & V. V. (Eds.), *Multi-Core Computer Vision and Image Processing for Intelligent Applications* (pp. 234-258). Hershey, PA: IGI Global. doi:10.4018/978-1-5225-0889-2.ch009

Saiz-Alvarez, J. M., & Leal, G. C. (2017). Cybersecurity Best Practices and Cultural Change in Global Business: Some Perspectives from the European Union. In G. Afolayan & A. Akinwale (Eds.), *Global Perspectives on Development Administration and Cultural Change* (pp. 48–73). Hershey, PA: IGI Global. doi:10.4018/978-1-5225-0629-4.ch003

Sang, Y., Zhu, Y., Zhao, H., & Tang, M. (2016). Study on an Interactive Truck Crane Simulation Platform Based on Virtual Reality Technology. *International Journal of Distance Education Technologies*, *14*(2), 64–78. doi:10.4018/IJDET.2016040105

Sarkar, D., & Roy, J. K. (2016). Artificial Neural Network (ANN) in Network Reconfiguration for Improvement of Voltage Stability. In S. Shandilya, S. Shandilya, T. Thakur, & A. Nagar (Eds.), *Handbook of Research on Emerging Technologies for Electrical Power Planning, Analysis, and Optimization* (pp. 184–206). Hershey, PA: IGI Global. doi:10.4018/978-1-4666-9911-3.ch010

Schafer, S. B. (2016). The Media-Sphere as Dream: Researching the Contextual Unconscious of Collectives. In S. Schafer (Ed.), *Exploring the Collective Unconscious in the Age of Digital Media* (pp. 232–260). Hershey, PA: IGI Global. doi:10.4018/978-1-4666-9891-8.ch010

Scheiter, K., & Eitel, A. (2017). The Use of Eye Tracking as a Research and Instructional Tool in Multimedia Learning. In C. Was, F. Sansosti, & B. Morris (Eds.), *Eye-Tracking Technology Applications in Educational Research* (pp. 143–164). Hershey, PA: IGI Global. doi:10.4018/978-1-5225-1005-5.ch008

Schneegass, S., Olsson, T., Mayer, S., & van Laerhoven, K. (2016). Mobile Interactions Augmented by Wearable Computing: A Design Space and Vision. *International Journal of Mobile Human Computer Interaction, 8*(4), 104–114. doi:10.4018/IJMHCI.2016100106

Shah, Z., & Kolhe, A. (2017). Throughput Analysis of IEEE 802.11ac and IEEE 802.11n in a Residential Home Environment. *International Journal of Interdisciplinary Telecommunications and Networking, 9*(1), 1–13. doi:10.4018/IJITN.2017010101

Shaqrah, A. A. (2016). Future of Smart Cities in the Knowledge-based Urban Development and the Role of Award Competitions. *International Journal of Knowledge-Based Organizations, 6*(1), 49–59. doi:10.4018/IJKBO.2016010104

Shayan, S., Abrahamson, D., Bakker, A., Duijzer, C. A., & van der Schaaf, M. (2017). Eye-Tracking the Emergence of Attentional Anchors in a Mathematics Learning Tablet Activity. In C. Was, F. Sansosti, & B. Morris (Eds.), *Eye-Tracking Technology Applications in Educational Research* (pp. 166–194). Hershey, PA: IGI Global. doi:10.4018/978-1-5225-1005-5.ch009

Sosnin, P. I. (2017). Conceptual Experiments in Automated Designing. In R. Zuanon (Ed.), *Projective Processes and Neuroscience in Art and Design* (pp. 155–181). Hershey, PA: IGI Global. doi:10.4018/978-1-5225-0510-5.ch010

Starostenko, O., Cruz-Perez, C., Alarcon-Aquino, V., Melnik, V. I., & Tyrsa, V. (2017). Machine Vision Application on Science and Industry: Real-Time Face Sensing and Recognition in Machine Vision – Trends and New Advances. In O. Sergiyenko & J. Rodriguez-Quiñonez (Eds.), *Developing and Applying Optoelectronics in Machine Vision* (pp. 146–179). Hershey, PA: IGI Global. doi:10.4018/978-1-5225-0632-4.ch005

Stasolla, F., Boccasini, A., & Perilli, V. (2017). Assistive Technology-Based Programs to Support Adaptive Behaviors by Children with Autism Spectrum Disorders: A Literature Overview. In Y. Kats (Ed.), *Supporting the Education of Children with Autism Spectrum Disorders* (pp. 140–159). Hershey, PA: IGI Global. doi:10.4018/978-1-5225-0816-8.ch008

Stratigea, A., Leka, A., & Panagiotopoulou, M. (2017). In Search of Indicators for Assessing Smart and Sustainable Cities and Communities Performance. *International Journal of E-Planning Research*, 6(1), 43–73. doi:10.4018/IJEPR.2017010103

Su, S., Lin, H. K., Wang, C., & Huang, Z. (2016). Multi-Modal Affective Computing Technology Design the Interaction between Computers and Human of Intelligent Tutoring Systems. *International Journal of Online Pedagogy and Course Design*, 6(1), 13–28. doi:10.4018/IJOPCD.2016010102

Sun, X., May, A., & Wang, Q. (2017). Investigation of the Role of Mobile Personalisation at Large Sports Events. *International Journal of Mobile Human Computer Interaction*, 9(1), 1–15. doi:10.4018/IJMHCI.2017010101

Szopa, A. (2017). The Influence of Crowdsourcing Business Model into Artificial Intelligence. In R. Batko & A. Szopa (Eds.), *Strategic Imperatives and Core Competencies in the Era of Robotics and Artificial Intelligence* (pp. 15–28). Hershey, PA: IGI Global. doi:10.4018/978-1-5225-1656-9.ch002

Tokunaga, S., Tamamizu, K., Saiki, S., Nakamura, M., & Yasuda, K. (2017). VirtualCareGiver: Personalized Smart Elderly Care. *International Journal of Software Innovation*, 5(1), 30–43. doi:10.4018/IJSI.2017010103

Trabelsi, I., & Bouhlel, M. S. (2016). Comparison of Several Acoustic Modeling Techniques for Speech Emotion Recognition. *International Journal of Synthetic Emotions*, 7(1), 58–68. doi:10.4018/IJSE.2016010105

Truman, B. (2017). New Constructions for Understanding using Virtual Learning-Towards Transdisciplinarity. In A. Stricker, C. Calongne, B. Truman, & F. Arenas (Eds.), *Integrating an Awareness of Selfhood and Society into Virtual Learning* (pp. 316–334). Hershey, PA: IGI Global. doi:10.4018/978-1-5225-2182-2.ch019

Turner, J. O. (2016). Virtual Soar-Agent Implementations: Examples, Issues, and Speculations. In J. Turner, M. Nixon, U. Bernardet, & S. DiPaola (Eds.), *Integrating Cognitive Architectures into Virtual Character Design* (pp. 181–212). Hershey, PA: IGI Global. doi:10.4018/978-1-5225-0454-2.ch007

Urrea, C., & Uren, V. (2017). Technical Evaluation, Development, and Implementation of a Remote Monitoring System for a Golf Cart. In N. Dey, A. Ashour, & S. Acharjee (Eds.), *Applied Video Processing in Surveillance and Monitoring Systems* (pp. 220–243). Hershey, PA: IGI Global. doi:10.4018/978-1-5225-1022-2.ch010

Veerapathiran, N., & Anand, S. (2017). Reducing False Alarms in Vision-Based Fire Detection. In N. Dey, A. Ashour, & S. Acharjee (Eds.), *Applied Video Processing in Surveillance and Monitoring Systems* (pp. 263–290). Hershey, PA: IGI Global. doi:10.4018/978-1-5225-1022-2.ch012

Vorraber, W., Lichtenegger, G., Brugger, J., Gojmerac, I., Egly, M., Panzenböck, K., & Voessner, S. et al. (2016). Designing Information Systems to Facilitate Civil-Military Cooperation in Disaster Management. *International Journal of Distributed Systems and Technologies*, 7(4), 22–40. doi:10.4018/IJDST.2016100102

Vyas, D., Kröner, A., & Nijholt, A. (2016). From Mundane to Smart: Exploring Interactions with Smart Design Objects. *International Journal of Mobile Human Computer Interaction*, 8(1), 59–82. doi:10.4018/IJMHCI.2016010103

Wang, L., Li, C., & Wu, J. (2017). The Status of Research into Intention Recognition. In J. Wu (Ed.), *Improving the Quality of Life for Dementia Patients through Progressive Detection, Treatment, and Care* (pp. 201–221). Hershey, PA: IGI Global. doi:10.4018/978-1-5225-0925-7.ch010

Wang, Y., Valipour, M., & Zatarain, O. A. (2016). Quantitative Semantic Analysis and Comprehension by Cognitive Machine Learning. *International Journal of Cognitive Informatics and Natural Intelligence*, 10(3), 13–28. doi:10.4018/IJCINI.2016070102

Xie, L., Zheng, L., & Yang, G. (2017). Hybrid Integration Technology for Wearable Sensor Systems. In C. Reis & M. Maximiano (Eds.), *Internet of Things and Advanced Application in Healthcare* (pp. 98–137). Hershey, PA: IGI Global. doi:10.4018/978-1-5225-1820-4.ch004

Xing, B., & Gao, W. (2014). Overview of Computational Intelligence. In *Computational Intelligence in Remanufacturing* (pp. 18–36). Hershey, PA: IGI Global. doi:10.4018/978-1-4666-4908-8.ch002

Xu, R., Li, Z., Cui, P., Zhu, S., & Gao, A. (2016). A Geometric Dynamic Temporal Reasoning Method with Tags for Cognitive Systems. *International Journal of Software Science and Computational Intelligence*, 8(4), 43–59. doi:10.4018/IJSSCI.2016100103

Yamaguchi, T., Nishimura, T., & Takadama, K. (2016). Awareness Based Recommendation: Passively Interactive Learning System. *International Journal of Robotics Applications and Technologies*, 4(1), 83–99. doi:10.4018/IJRAT.2016010105

Zentall, S. R., & Junglen, A. G. (2017). Investigating Mindsets and Motivation through Eye Tracking and Other Physiological Measures. In C. Was, F. Sansosti, & B. Morris (Eds.), *Eye-Tracking Technology Applications in Educational Research* (pp. 48–64). Hershey, PA: IGI Global. doi:10.4018/978-1-5225-1005-5.ch003

Zielinska, T. (2016). Professional and Personal Service Robots. *International Journal of Robotics Applications and Technologies*, 4(1), 63–82. doi:10.4018/IJRAT.2016010104

Zohora, S. E., Khan, A. M., Srivastava, A. K., Nguyen, N. G., & Dey, N. (2016). A Study of the State of the Art in Synthetic Emotional Intelligence in Affective Computing. *International Journal of Synthetic Emotions*, 7(1), 1–12. doi:10.4018/IJSE.2016010101

Index

Stay Current on the Latest Emerging Research Developments

Become an IGI Global Reviewer for Authored Book Projects

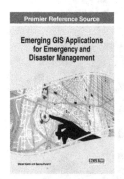

Premier Reference Source

Emerging GIS Applications for Emergency and Disaster Management

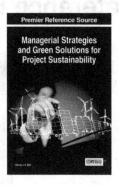

Premier Reference Source

Managerial Strategies and Green Solutions for Project Sustainability

Premier Reference Source

Comparative Approaches to Using R and Python for Statistical Data Analysis

Premier Reference Source

Solutions for High-Touch Communications in a High-Tech World

The overall success of an authored book project is dependent on quality and timely reviews.

In this competitive age of scholarly publishing, constructive and timely feedback significantly decreases the turnaround time of manuscripts from submission to acceptance, allowing the publication and discovery of progressive research at a much more expeditious rate. Several IGI Global authored book projects are currently seeking highly qualified experts in the field to fill vacancies on their respective editorial review boards:

Applications may be sent to:
development@igi-global.com

Applicants must have a doctorate (or an equivalent degree) as well as publishing and reviewing experience. Reviewers are asked to write reviews in a timely, collegial, and constructive manner. All reviewers will begin their role on an ad-hoc basis for a period of one year, and upon successful completion of this term can be considered for full editorial review board status, with the potential for a subsequent promotion to Associate Editor.

If you have a colleague that may be interested in this opportunity, we encourage you to share this information with them.

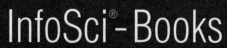
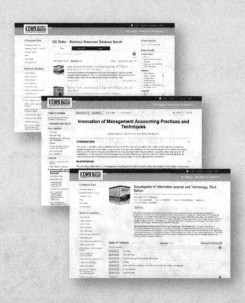

Printed in the United States
By Bookmasters